"I highly recommend *Called Out*! It is a heartfelt, funny, vulnerable guide to overcoming the pressure to 'win' at all costs, and instead live the life you were made for."

—Michael Strahan

"I had the pleasure to take a seat alongside Paula on *The View* for two years. *Called Out* is an honest look into the very thing that holds many of us back: fear. Paula explains that God can move us through those fears and into a deeper sense of both our faith calling and the calling of our career. If you want to pepper more peace, purpose, and balance into your life, this book is a wonderful place to start."

—Candace Cameron Bure, actress, producer, and *New York Times* bestselling author

"Paula's personal story of risking it all to pursue her God-given purpose will inspire you on your own journey of finding success God's way."

—Christine Caine, bestselling author and founder of A21 and Propel Women

"The way Paula unpacks her message that success doesn't define you hit me right in the heart. Filled with funny stories and fascinating insight into her career, *Called Out* is a much needed love letter to working moms everywhere—and Paula is one I continue to look up to!"

—Rachel Cruze, #1 *New York Times* bestselling author and host of *The Rachel Cruze Show*

"We sometimes think of *calling* and *career* as the same thing, but Paula Faris does a beautiful job shining a light on the differences, helping us understand that our work isn't our worth."

—T. D. Jakes Sr., senior pastor/CEO, The Potter's House/TDJ Enterprises

"My friend Paula combines a raw, compelling personal story with an urgent question faced by so many of us: How do we make sure our professional choices line up with our professed values? Countless people will benefit from the bravery Paula exhibits in this book."

—Dan Harris, ABC News anchor/correspondent and author of *10% Happier*

"So many people feel trapped trying to follow the path of success yet know that something significant is missing. Paula Faris has written a gut-wrenchingly transparent book entitled *Called Out: Why I Traded Two Dream Jobs for a Life of True Calling*. If you feel stuck and are longing for more, Paula's encouraging story will stir your spirit, move your heart, and build your faith to believe you can discover a divine calling instead of simply pursuing a career."

—Craig Groeschel, pastor of Life.Church
and *New York Times* bestselling author

"In this compelling book, Paula makes herself vulnerable in order to enlighten us—not just about the perils of burnout, but about anything in our lives that gets in the way of us becoming all we were meant to be."

—Melissa Joan Hart

"Paula is incurably curious. She asks astounding questions (I know this firsthand), and she is a wellspring of good advice. (Again, I speak from personal experience.) Most of all, she is in dogged pursuit of a life that lives out faith and values. If you desire to do the same, then you are holding the right book. It is well written and inviting. The ideas are timely and timeless. Thank you, Paula, for sharing them with us."

—from the afterword by Max Lucado, pastor
and bestselling author of *How Happiness Happens*

"Paula is a modern-day working mama who inspires me with her candor and wit! She makes the tough calls, advocates for the next generation, and lives a life of courageous faith. In these pages you'll find clarity on how to embrace your true calling and the courage to take the next step!"

—Rebekah Lyons, author, *Rhythms of Renewal* and *You Are Free*

"In *Called Out*, Paula Faris does a fabulous job of using her personal struggles with career, expectations, and purpose to encourage readers to push past their fears and step into their true calling."

—Meghan McCain, co-host of *The View*

"Whether you're just stepping into the job market or you're a vocational veteran, *Called Out* has something for you. Paula's honest look at work and life is refreshing. More important, it reminds us to stop fooling ourselves and to start anchoring our lives in the things that really matter."

—Dave Ramsey, bestselling author and nationally syndicated
radio show host

"It is so easy to be defined by a job, by a title, or by worldly accolades. And yet, God calls us to a purpose so much higher. Paula's story is such a relatable and inspiring example of this. If you are wrestling through a season of transition, this is the book for you."

—Tim Tebow

CALLED OUT

CALLED OUT

Why I Traded Two Dream Jobs for a Life of True Calling

PAULA FARIS

BETHANYHOUSE
a division of Baker Publishing Group
Minneapolis, Minnesota

Published by Bethany House Publishers
11400 Hampshire Avenue South
Bloomington, Minnesota 55438
www.bethanyhouse.com

Bethany House Publishers is a division of
Baker Publishing Group, Grand Rapids, Michigan

Printed in the United States of America

ISBN 978-0-7642-3543-6 (cloth)
ISBN 978-0-7642-3544-3 (paperback)

Library of Congress Cataloging-in-Publication Control Number: 2019955193

Unless otherwise indicated, Scripture quotations are from the Holy Bible, New International Version®. NIV®. Copyright © 1973, 1978, 1984, 2011 by Biblica, Inc.™ Used by permission of Zondervan. All rights reserved worldwide. www.zondervan.com. The "NIV" and "New International Version" are trademarks registered in the United States Patent and Trademark Office by Biblica, Inc.™

Scripture quotations identified ESV are from The Holy Bible, English Standard Version® (ESV®), copyright © 2001 by Crossway, a publishing ministry of Good News Publishers. Used by permission. All rights reserved. ESV Text Edition: 2016

Scripture quotations identified KJV are from the King James Version of the Bible.

Scripture quotations identified MESSAGE are from THE MESSAGE, copyright © 1993, 1994, 1995, 1996, 2000, 2001, 2002 by Eugene H. Peterson. Used by permission of NavPress. All rights reserved. Represented by Tyndale House Publishers, Inc.

Scripture quotations identified NKJV are from the New King James Version®. Copyright © 1982 by Thomas Nelson. Used by permission. All rights reserved.

Scripture quotations identified TPT are from The Passion Translation®. Copyright © 2017 by BroadStreet Publishing® Group, LLC. Used by permission. All rights reserved. thePassionTranslation.com

This book recounts events in the life of Paula Faris according to the author's recollection and information from the author's perspective. While all stories are true, some dialogue and identifying details have been changed to protect the privacy of the people involved.

Cover design by LOOK Design Studio
Cover photography by Heidi Gutman-Guillaume

Author is represented by United Talent Agency.

20 21 22 23 24 25 26   7 6 5 4 3 2 1

For my dad . . . I love you forever.

CONTE

N T S

CHAPTER 1

News Anchor Kills Career Over Burger and Fries

There's no rational way to kill your career. This is my last thought before walking from the shadows of the ABC News headquarters' redbrick façade on West 66th Street in New York City. But after six years, hundreds of interviews, thousands of hours filing reports for the network and co-hosting *World News Now*, countless hours hosting the weekend edition of *Good Morning America* (*GMA*), and taking my seat on *The View*, it's time. I'm ready to pull the trigger, and if I don't, I know my addiction will get the best of me.

Stepping onto Columbus Avenue, I throw my sunglasses on, flip open the notepad in my hand, and ignore the first signs of spring budding from the trees, pushing up from the street-side planters, and sprouting up from the window boxes of Lincoln Center. It's the right kind of day for hard conversations, the spring sun smiling down on the Upper West Side of Manhattan, and as I walk, I study my notes and rehearse my lines. I've rehearsed them a hundred times—at home, in the car, in the bathroom, at the office. I've made my husband, John, suffer through my practice sessions. But this time, I'm not preparing for a TV appearance. This time, I'm preparing for the most important conversation of my career.

Rubbing shoulders with someone who'd refused to yield my side of the sidewalk—or had I crossed into hers?—I don't look up or apologize or make eye contact. Instead, I head south toward the Atlantic Grill restaurant, right fist balled up, flicking my wrist for emphasis as I tick off the bullet points. I tune out the street noise, the hissing of a stopping bus, the sounds of sirens, a person talking to a hot dog vendor. I can't forget a single word on this note pad.

I turn the corner to West 65th and as I do, my heart flutters and a hole opens up in my stomach. *I'm really doing this*, I think. Regardless of how much it scares me. I see the back entrance for the Atlantic Grill, a local hangout for journalists and news executives, and I pray no one else from the network is in there chowing down cheeseburgers with a side of gossip. I'd rather not be the subject of more rumors.

Through the door, I nod to the host and tell him I'm meeting James Goldston. Mr. Goldston hasn't arrived, he says. I thank him, letting him know I'll be back after running to the ladies' room. In the restroom, I stand directly in front of the mirror and give myself a little pep talk.

You know what you want.
Stay firm in your demands.
Even though he scheduled this meeting, you are in the driver's seat.
Don't let your fear get the best of you.

12

I check my hair, my glasses, my blouse. I look the part—confident, strong journalist—no matter how fast my heart pounds. I repeat the salient points to myself one last time: It's been a trying season (*no, a year of hell*) and I've worked through it all; the hours have been insane and there's no end in sight (*should I bring up the twenty-one straight shifts without a break?*); John and I haven't been able to take time off in years (*does this sound too whiny?*); God seems to be drawing me in a different direction (*careful not to over-spiritualize it, Paula*). I repeat the phrases, then put the notes down and try to recite them by memory, but my brain is at capacity, my thoughts muddled. I'd do anything for a teleprompter.

When I return to the dining room, the host leads me back to my table and takes my drink order. Water is fine, I say, then place my cheat sheet to my right while I wait for James to make his entrance. When he walks through the double doors of the Atlantic Grill, heads turn. Even if he weren't the president of ABC News, he'd attract attention. Tall, slender, and in his mid-fifties, he carries himself with purpose. And a smile. It's an easy smile, the kind that's a rarity among Manhattan movers and shakers. He walks kindly, if such a thing is possible, and I suspect this is what's made James an accomplished journalist.

I scoot out of the booth to give him a hug, and he tells me it's good to see me. I slide back into my seat, and once he is centered against the cherry-red leather back of the booth, he launches into the usual pleasantries.

How's John? Is he still enjoying commercial real estate?

What about the kids? Is Caroline doing well in school?

How old is Landon now? Has he started soccer yet?

I answer his questions and ask him a few of my own. James tells me about his wife, his three boys, and how much they are loving soccer. Speaking of soccer, we launch into a conversation about the international leagues. We play conversational tennis—a skill successful broadcasting professionals hone to a fine point—and as we do, I almost forget the pit in my stomach and the fact that my hands tremble as I pick up my water glass.

I'm almost at ease, but then I remember why we're here. He has called this meeting to discuss my contract, and consequently, my future with the network. I pivot from the chitchat and create space to have a more meaningful conversation.

"So," I say, opening the conversational door. James walks through.

"We know it's been a tough season," he says, "but we don't want you to walk away from the ABC family. We love your work, your attitude, the joy you bring to the studio. What'll it take to keep you around?"

I glance at my notepad one last time, taking stock of the bullet points. How forceful can I be? How assertive? What if I say it all wrong? What if I'm too much? I imagine the headline: "News Anchor Kills Career Over Burger and Fries." But James already knows my struggles, my needs, even my demands. We're a part of the ABC family, and for better or worse, it's the kind of family that doesn't keep secrets well (after all, many journalists make a name for themselves by outing other people's secrets). He wants to hear it straight from the horse's mouth, though, and knowing it's now or never, all or nothing, I dive headfirst into the topic *du jour*.

> "I don't think God's calling me to sacrifice my family for my career."

"James, if ABC wants me to stay, I need to walk away from *The View* and the weekend anchor desk at *GMA*. The Wednesday-through-Sunday schedule is killing me. It's starting to affect my marriage. It's keeping me from my kids, and I don't think God's calling me to sacrifice my family for my career."

He nods but says nothing.

"Keeping the same schedule is an absolute nonstarter."

He nods again, says he understands, but I'm just getting started. I look at my cheat sheet, gathering my thoughts and my breath as I launch into a more detailed explanation.

"This isn't a rash decision," I say, though James never said it was. "It's been a year in the making." He nods, reaches for his water and takes a long drink. I give him more history than he's asked for and tell him I tried to step back last year.

"You did?" he asks.

"You don't remember my conversation?"

"Vaguely. Remind me."

I take him through a meeting I'd had the year before with another ABC executive, in which I had shared how the job was taking its toll, and recounted all my struggles on *The View*—how I'd been in the tricky position of attempting to be a neutral journalist on the show's panel while trying not to out my own political leanings, which would affect my career as a balanced and impartial journalist. It had created tension with some of my co-hosts, I said, and when I'd tried to step back from the turmoil, I suffered a bout of negative press through various tabloids. The "reporting" had been unfounded, untruthful, and unfair—unfortunately, in my business, this comes with the territory. My schedule had been out of whack too, and there'd been multiple stretches when I'd worked almost a month straight without a single day off. All this stress and pressure led to deteriorating health, and I had told the executive that too. I'd suffered on-air asthma attacks that nearly led to on-air panic attacks. And this was to say nothing of how I felt about my growing family disconnection with John and the kids. They were getting my leftovers—leftover time, leftover energy, leftover joy. It wasn't right, I'd told the executive.

James listens as I recount the story, then asks what his colleague had said in response.

"What any good boss would say: that I'd be crazy to leave, that it would hurt my career, maybe even set me back in the long term."

That executive had reminded me I'd been given opportunities that other people would kill for. I'd risen from a relatively small market in Ohio and, according to the executive, with my talent and tenacity, there was nowhere to go but up. I was a rising star, and walking away from the co-anchor desk would change the trajectory of my career, might hurt the assignments I received, I was told. Besides, if I kept working at the same clip interviewing the top politicians and celebrities, if I kept chasing down big stories, if I kept delivering as a co-anchor, my opportunities were limitless. The executive made a compelling case. As I listened, as I considered, it felt as if I were being dragged away from whatever resolve I'd had.

I could have been angry about this, I tell James, but I wasn't. That executive was just doing their job, trying to protect me from sabotaging myself—and from a certain perspective, was right. Still, this person hadn't lived in my shoes for the last year, and I hadn't shared my struggles with this person until that meeting, so I didn't cast blame for not knowing how broken and vulnerable I felt.

As I tell James the story, the words echoed in my head: *"You'd be crazy . . ."*

I chewed on those words.

"I don't blame the exec," I reiterate. "After all, they weren't the only one."

Just days before, when I'd told Dan Harris—my weekend *GMA* co-anchor and close friend—that I was considering leaving the co-anchor desk, he'd said much the same thing, that I was crazy to step away from both the career and the people I loved. (He supported me 100 percent once I explained my reasoning.) But the executive went a step further than Dan, warning me of the long-term vocational implications. And although just looking out for my career, the exec didn't know just how much fear their comments incited—didn't know I had a history of letting fear dictate my decisions. That exec didn't know how the conversation had revved up my internal dialogue.

If I walked away, would I be considered a failure?

If I took time off, would I ever make it back to the big stage?

Would people think I was too weak to hack it or that I was forced out?

Worse yet, if I wasn't in the spotlight, would I even know who I was?

I tell James that it was the fear that changed my mind, that kept me from stepping back. It was the fear that made me dig in. Stick it out. Work harder. What a mistake—one I was ready to own a year later.

I stop blabbering long enough to shove a bite into my mouth and wash it down with water. James responds, remembering the conversation now, at least in part. He hadn't realized how serious I'd been, though. I guess I hadn't either, I say, staring down at my burger. But this last year—my year from hell—had gotten my attention.

I take James through the hardest year of my adult life, one made all the more difficult because leading up to it, I thought I was in the clear. The rough season on *The View* had smoothed out, and despite burning the candle at both ends, I'd enjoyed it. I had a full portfolio of big interviews, with folks like Kim Davis, the controversial county clerk of Rowan County, Kentucky, who refused to issue marriage licenses to gay couples after same-sex marriage was legalized by the United States Supreme Court in 2015. I had interviewed several of the Duggar children about coping with the sex scandal involving their brother Josh Duggar, who their parents admitted had molested five girls, including four of his underaged sisters. I'd interviewed Hillary Clinton, Bernie Sanders, and Joe Biden on *The View.* I had covered the Election Day results out of the swing state of Florida in November 2016. And in September of 2017, I'd landed an exclusive interview with Sean Spicer just after his controversial Emmy Awards appearance. And to put the cherry on top of it all, I'd found out I was pregnant with our fourth child. But in September of 2017, the winds seemed to shift. In fact, it was as if a tornado touched down.

First was the miscarriage, I tell him. Then an emergency surgery due to an infection from the miscarriage. Through it all, I hadn't slowed down. I couldn't tell James why I hadn't taken a break, really. But the reason was fear. Fear that I would let people down, or that I might have to deal with the grief. Maybe I was afraid the grief would turn to despair. Ultimately, though, I was afraid of living without my narcotic of choice—work.

James offers a comforting, "You could have stepped away for a while, Paula. We would have understood."

I know, I say, but I don't think it was so much about them as it was about me. I pause, wondering if that sounds like some cheesy breakup line. (Yep, pretty sure it does.) Then I launch back into Hell Year, tell James the hits just kept coming after the miscarriage. There had been the incident outside the Stock Exchange, when an apple hurled by a pedestrian exploded against the side of my head just seconds before I was going live for *Good Morning America*. I remind him of the concussion that apple-sode caused, of how it sidelined me for weeks. Then there was the head-on car wreck the day I'd been cleared to return to work. (Even as I tell James the story, it's hard to believe.) Still, after each time, I rolled back to the studio as soon as I could, sometimes still in a fog, sometimes not remembering who I'd interviewed the day before. (Had I really interviewed Jimmy Kimmel on *The View*? There was footage to prove that I had, but I had no recollection of it.) But when the worst case of influenza hit me, then turned into pneumonia, I knew I was either struggling through a season of "bad karma," or God was trying to send me a message. In less than seven months I'd had five major events, each of which seemed to point to the fact that I had to slow down.

In less than seven months, I'd had five major events, each of which seemed to point to the fact that I had to slow down.

I say it all to James, and even as I do, I realize how crazy I sound, and not because I think God is conspiring with the universe to try to send me a message. I sound crazy because I'm afraid of taking a break, walking away, finding an identity that's not rooted in my ability to bounce back from adversity and dive back into work, regardless of how much I'm hurting myself or others. Am I an addict? The question fully forms, though I don't admit it to James, and that's when I catch a small whisper.

Be still, Paula.

Slow down.

Find rest in me.

Find who you are in me.

I've spoken my piece, and I take a breath. I remembered all the points, and the panic hadn't set in. The air in the Atlantic Grill seems lighter, sweeter. James has taken in every word, offering empathetic *mm-hmms* along the way. He is a colleague, but sitting across the table from me, he seems more like an uncle or a brother now. And though I half expect him to argue with me, to tell me I need to stick it out for a few more years or keep climbing the ladder for a while, though I half expect him to promise me more opportunity, he doesn't. Instead, he smiles.

"You can't leave," he says matter of factly. "You're too important to this family. But that doesn't mean we can't make some changes. Do you know what you want?"

Did I know what I wanted? A great question, the short answer to which was *sort of*. The hole in my stomach fills with excited electricity. I want the calling of my faith and the calling of my vocation to align, but how do I say this?

"I want to cover the consequential stories. I want the big interviews. More Spicer interviews. More stories like the Roy Moore scandal in Alabama. I want to chase the stories where politics, life, and religion intersect too. I've been thinking it'd be great to have an ABC faith podcast, a place where my faith might direct some of the content. And I want to do it all on the weekdays. No more weekends."

James catches my energy, sees my enthusiasm. It sounds doable, he says as he slides his credit card out of the black bifold bill holder on the table and signs the receipt. It actually sounds amazing, he says.

We slide out of the booth, and James offers me another hug, thanking me for shooting straight. He's running late for another meeting, he says, but we should keep talking. I assure him we will, and we turn our separate ways, he toward the front door, I toward the back.

On the sidewalk outside the Atlantic Grill, I see the city for the first time that day. The leaves of the trees springing up from the sidewalk are bright green. A man walks his dog past me. A woman passes with a grocery bag. I turn toward Columbus Avenue, toward a great mass of people driving and taxiing and walking. Who are these people? Do they know themselves and what they want, or are they so wrapped up in their careers that they have time for nothing else? Does fear keep them from stepping away, taking a break, slowing down, or exploring new vocational opportunities? Are they as I was a year ago, as I still am, even now? Are any of us all that different?

I reach for my phone, but then decide against it. I'll call John later, maybe when I figure out how I feel about my lunch conversation with James. And anyway, if I pulled out my phone, would I even call him? Wouldn't I get sucked back into the vortex of work emails and texts? That's the way I normally deal with fear, with ambiguity; I turn straight to work. Not now. Not today.

At the intersection of 65th and Columbus, I remember words attributed to Dr. Martin Luther King: "Faith is taking the first step, even when you don't see the whole staircase." I guess this is why faith is so difficult for me, and for so many others. What if that staircase leads to nowhere? What if there's no next step at all and we fall off a cliff? And truth be told, I couldn't even see that first step. But the arc of my life reminds me that all those what-ifs are nonsense. I've been plagued by fear my whole life—fear of failure, fear of not fitting in, fear of being alone, fear of being embarrassed, fear that I didn't belong, fear that I wasn't good enough—and over the years, I'd almost lost myself to those fears. But time after time, God moved me through those fears and into a deeper sense of my callings, both my faith calling and the calling of my career.

When I was a teenager, he walked me through the fear and into a new season of calling.

In my first year of college, he walked me through the fear and into a new season of calling.

After 9/11, he walked me through the fear and into a new season of vocational calling.

As he'd been with Moses, he'd always been with me. He'd parted seas for me, led me to the right people at the right times. Right?

Columbus Avenue comes into view, and the truth falls on me like a piano dropped from the apartment window six stories above me: I really was crazy to take this step back.

What had I just done?

At the corner, I take a deep breath and lock eyes with a stranger. We smile at each other, and she offers me a good afternoon. I don't know where she's going, but I'm headed into a season of ambiguity, I guess. Relief holds one hand. Fear holds the other.

Calling, Career, and Vocation—The Buzzwords of an Age

We're inundated with messages on a daily basis.

"Live with purpose; walk in your calling," our pastors, priests, rabbis, and other faith leaders preach.

"Focus on the next achievable goal," our business leaders teach.

"Live with intention," the self-help gurus instruct.

Calling, purpose, focus, intention, balance are the buzzwords of our time. Forget about how to achieve those things—what do they even mean? And what if we're purposed, focused, and intent on pursuing the wrong thing? Will our lives be full of meaning? Will they be out of balance?

For years I thought I was living with purpose, focus, and intention as I followed my broadcasting career from Ohio all the way to the Big Apple. God had given me opportunity after opportunity and, committed to my vocation as I was, I put my head down and gave everything to those opportunities. I did my best to follow the best advice of the spiritual leaders, the business insiders, and the self-help gurus. I thought that climbing the ranks meant I was achieving, that by all accounts, I was successful. Didn't society say as much? But if that was true, why did it feel as if I was letting everyone down? Why did I feel like John, my kids, my friends, and my church were getting my leftovers?

There were years I felt the tension and guilt, years I was afraid of stepping back and squandering my opportunities, but God has a way of disrupting unhealthy lifestyles, just as he did mine. Yet even as I walked out of the Atlantic Grill without any real plan, I still wasn't sure what God wanted to teach me. I didn't know he'd set me on a path of spiritual discovery, or that those discoveries would come through a series of interviews and life-altering loss. In fact, I didn't even know I needed new spiritual discoveries. All I knew was that walking away from the anchor desk felt simultaneously like freedom and the loss of my identity. It felt a little like hope and failure. And it was the freedom and loss of identity, the hope and failure, that exposed a deep fear.

Did I even know myself without this career?

Could I?

My worth had become my work.

My value, in my vocation.

Maybe you have been there too. Maybe you are there now. Maybe you've done your best to follow your vocational calling as a teacher, doctor, or stay-at-home mom, but somehow it doesn't quite feel right. You haven't found your fit, don't feel like you're living a life of purpose, one firmly rooted in an identity outside of what you do, your day-to-day vocation, day-to-day life. Like me, maybe you're afraid to reexamine your vocational calling, afraid to explore whether you're being called to something different, something more fulfilling, more whole. Maybe you're afraid to walk away from what you do because you have no idea who you are without it. If you've been there, if you're there now, I'm glad you're reading this book.

When I first sat down to put my thoughts on paper, I was a little (maybe even a lot) on edge. I was still sorting out my journey, still a little out of sorts. I wasn't sure I knew who I was without anchoring the weekend edition of *GMA* and co-hosting *The View*, though I knew I'd better sort it out. And as a journalist, I knew the best way to sort out any story was to start investigating, start exploring, start asking questions and peeling back the layers, and that's exactly what I did. I began interviewing people for my faith podcast, and so often

Maybe you're afraid to walk away from what you do because you have no idea who you are without it. If you've been there, if you're there now, I'm glad you're reading this book.

the conversation turned to questions of calling, questions we all have. I read articles, books, and stories of people doing their best to sort out vocational questions—*what was it they were born to do?* In the months after my dad passed, I pored over his notes and journals, read the words of a man who was ever centered in his calling, one who gained his identity from who he was and not what he did. And as I researched, as I compiled a journalist's notebook, I came to see some truths about our calling, about the fear that limits those callings, and about the rooted identity that helps us push through the fear. This book is the culmination of my journalist's notebook on calling, purpose, and identity.

As you read along, I hope you'll explore the similarities between my life, yours, and the lives of those I've interviewed. Sure, you're probably not a Midwestern radio-sales-girl-turned-news-anchor, or an international spy, or a megachurch preacher, or a United States Marine. But the circumstances of your journey are as unique as my own, and if you're anything like me, you might find yourself wanting more clarity on the direction of your vocational calling. (And yes, vocational calling includes being a stay-at-home mom, which is one of the toughest.) You might find yourself wanting more alignment between who you say you are and what you do. And hopefully it won't take getting hit upside the head with an apple to slow you down long enough to examine that alignment. (I hope it doesn't, because it hurts like Hades.)

If you feel a little lost in your vocation, if you feel as if you wouldn't know yourself outside of *what you do*, if you don't even know what you're called to do vocationally, if you're too scared to take a vocational leap of faith, or if you just want to find more peace, purpose, and balance in your day-to-day life, this book is for you. As you read, I hope you'll find a new way forward. More than anything, I hope you'll discover the true vine from which your vocational calling grows—your faith calling.

What is your faith calling?

Let's find out.

CHAPTER 2

Girl Misses Her Faith Calling, Settles for Drug of Choice—Success

I come from a line of self-doubters turned self-starters. I come from a roll-up-your-sleeves and put-your-nose-to-the-grindstone people. I come from tenacious agitators hell-bent on proving they fit in. I come from a line of immigrants. (As Lin-Manuel Miranda said, "We get the job done!")

My dad, Ed Faris, was a first-generation American, the product of Lebanese immigrants who had fled their home country in search of a better life. Gido (his father, my grandpa) was a hard man and an even harder worker, a taskmaster who demanded adherence to family obligations. Sito, my grandma, was the gentler, more spiritual, more nurturing type. But as different as they could be, they shared one nonnegotiable: They, and anyone living in their home, were obligated to attend the Maronite Catholic Church every Sunday morning.

It's hard to say how connected Gido and my dad were, but all the evidence suggests their relationship was emotionally stunted. Gido was a firm disciplinarian; his words were harsh and his belt stung, and this made the going rough on my dad. So when my dad was old enough to make his own decisions, he fled the coop, setting out to blaze his own trail in a land full of opportunities. And for a while, that included wandering away from the faith of his family.

Opportunities—my dad made the most of them. A young patriot, Dad showed loyalty to his new country by joining the Marines. Academically inclined, he enrolled in the engineering program at the University of Michigan, and after he graduated, he received his master's degree in electrical engineering. (Go Blue!) He joined the workforce and went all in, setting his sights on climbing the corporate ladder. Through all of it, he pursued other opportunities too, particularly any associated with a good party.

After graduating from the University of Michigan, Dad took a job with McDonnell Aircraft, which landed him in St. Louis, Missouri. Looking for a good time and a pretty girl, he attended a dance at the Catholic Alumni Club in the summer of 1964. He was a nominal Catholic at best—religion was the only opportunity he didn't really make the most of—and his faith wasn't active outside the occasional outing to a Catholic dance in an effort to score a potential date. But that night, Dad met Carol Kostecki, a straitlaced, newly minted Catholic school graduate who'd only broken her commitment to join the Peace Corps because her family needed her to stay home and make a little extra income. She was a do-gooder. A self-described prude. Anything but a black sheep. She was my dad's opposite.

If my dad were still alive—he passed during the writing of this book—he'd tell you my mom was a beauty inside and out, the kind of girl any young Catholic man would dream of taking home to his parents. Her goodness was enough to make anyone want to get right, and her looks didn't hurt either. They danced that summer night, and though my mom wasn't immediately taken with my dad's square jaw and dark olive skin—she didn't agree to a date after that first dance— they found each other again at a similar dance that winter. That's where the sparks flew. (As my mom later said, "By the winter of 1965, he was looking pretty good.") And after dating only a few months, my dad popped the question a little awkwardly: "Carol, will you think about marrying me?"

My parents were married in 1966 at my mom's home church, St. Francis De Sales, in St. Louis. Four months later, and not even a year into their relationship, they were pregnant with their first child, my sister Dianne. Thirteen months later my sister Mary came along. Then, in 1972, my older brother, Dan, was born. As the family grew, the responsibility did too. And through it all, my dad kept pressing, kept trying to do more, be more, achieve more. He charged harder at work, put in later hours in his attempt to do more, to prove he could give the family what it needed. He charged hard at home too; he laid down the law and expected the family to follow it, just as his father had.

All that hard charging, though, took its toll—at least that's what the psychologist wrote.

After my dad died, I found a box of documents he had saved in his office. Journalist that I am, innately curious as I am (okay, I'll admit I'm nosy), I dove into that box, and in it I found a report from Scientific Associates Consulting for Industry and Education, a firm that provided a psychological evaluation of my dad in 1971. After a thorough evaluation, the psychologist concluded that my dad had an IQ of 130 (which is knocking on the door of genius level), that he could "think critically, probably right along with the best." But despite his intelligence and the frequent references to his "fine mind" and capability for "intellectual growth," the doctor noted, "[Ed Faris] does not appear to be too calm and has showed some signs of anxiety. . . . He might be a little insecure. This could be a motivating factor in his favor, however."

Plagued by insecurity and anxiety, my dad soon found that no amount of success made him feel any better. *So he did what many men in stressful careers with growing families and mounting pressures do: He began searching for relief.* He attended a Transcendental Meditation class, where he fell asleep and was prodded awake when he started snoring. (It's just like my dad to ruin a good meditation with snoring.) Unmoved, embarrassed, and given the cold shoulder by the group of meditators, he never returned. What he didn't find in meditation, he searched for by trying valium, but that didn't bring peace either, at least not the lasting peace he was looking for. He must have been growing desperate, because after several invitations from his boss to visit a multidenominational Christian Bible study that met upstairs at the Catholic church on Sunday nights, my dad accepted.

The group was known as Morning Star Christian Community, a community of faith that sprung from the charismatic renewal of the 1970s. They gathered people from various churches across the Jackson, Michigan, area. Together, they comprised one family of faith—a family committed to prayer, worship, and most important, each other. But it wasn't just about the Sunday worship experience. The group had a specific and defined purpose: to live in unity despite their religious differences or preferences, and to focus on making God known to the community.

It took only one visit for Dad to feel the warmth, care, and sense of peace and calm he had been looking for. The people seemed to accept him for who he was—a child of God—and not for what he did. So the next week, he asked my mom to attend while he kept the kids, in hopes that she'd experience the same warmth, care, and sense of peace. She wasn't keen on the idea and held out for weeks, but she finally agreed to go. Once she did, she was just as taken, felt just as drawn into the community. From that Sunday on, my parents became committed members of the Morning Star Christian Community.

They continued to attend their Catholic church on Sunday mornings (the church where I would later take my First Communion), and they took the family to Morning Star on Sunday nights. The Morning Star community came alongside them, helped them understand who they were in God, and taught them how to build a God-honoring marriage and home. Dad began making dinnertime a priority, and he softened around the house too. Though he was still firm in his discipline, he was more connected emotionally, more loving, more grace-filled. He lived with more peace, even if he still struggled with his self-esteem from time to time. My mom would later tell me in an impromptu interview in a coffee shop (yes, I interview family members, friends, and my kids in my free time), that the changes couldn't have come at a better time. Had they stayed the course they'd set prior to Morning Star, she said, they'd have surely ended up divorced. The community at Morning Star had saved their marriage.

By the autumn of 1975, my parents were on their way to building a thriving marriage, and it was into this environment that I made my appearance. Though we'd eventually move from the Catholic church to a local Lutheran church, the Morning Star Community was our constant. (In fact, it has remained a constant in my mom's life, even after my dad's death.) My parents continued to deepen in their faith and began taking things like prayer and Bible study seriously. Dad studied the Bible every morning—couldn't get enough of it. He prayed with Mom every day. Together, they served their community of faith and offered whatever they could when a need arose.

They took holiness seriously too. There was no trick-or-treating (Halloween was the devil's holiday); my sisters and I couldn't wear skirts above the knees; I wasn't allowed to watch movies that weren't approved by Movie Morality Guide (movie reviews from a Christian perspective); and I was taken out of sex-ed class in junior high. But this isn't to say that my parents were prudes. They enjoyed wine and beer in moderation, normally having a glass or two at dinner. From time to time, they'd let us take a sip too. (I remember my first sip of beer at the ripe old age of five.)

Though the pendulum swung pretty far to the right in the realm of modesty, entertainment, holiday celebrations, and sexuality, and most people would categorize my upbringing as "fundamentalist," I never doubted how much my parents loved me. I never doubted that they were for me, that they believed in me, and that they wanted the best for my life. I never doubted that they were doing the best they could with the information they had. After all, they were still trying to figure it all out too.

That said, one problem I did have with my fundamentalist upbringing was that I never felt like I was quite good enough, even if no one told me as much. My actions followed that feeling. I couldn't focus long enough during my mandatory daily devotion time, so on more than one occasion, I sneaked out my window and spent time with friends. I didn't want to be considered a prude, so in my teenage years, a friend and I hid in the A-frame fort my dad built for me in the backyard, and we smoked cigarettes lifted when their parents weren't looking. (Sorry, Mr. and Mrs. Young!)

I never met an authority I didn't want to question, and "Why?" became my default question for everything. If the answer wasn't sufficient, I'd ask again. And again. This, I guess, was how I came to earn the nickname "Paula 20 Questions."

If I'd felt inadequate only at home, that might have been okay. But the feelings of inadequacy followed me to school. And that's where my self-esteem took the biggest hit. I was a normal-sized girl with unusually large green eyes. To make matters worse, I dressed like a character from 1950s movies, all modest blouses and below-the-knee skirts, and so I became the target of ridicule for my public-school peers. They teased me as I walked down the hall, calling me "Paula fish eyes" or "guppy." In the lunchroom, they spoofed the song Ernie used to sing on *Sesame Street*, taunting, "Guppy, guppy, you're the one; you make bath time lots of fun. . . ." On more occasions than not, I walked to my mom's car at the end of the day, head down, dragging. Sometimes there were tears.

In my high school years, I began to drift. A directionless wandering was setting in, and though I believed in God, though I did my best to be a good Christian girl, it didn't seem to provide me with the same sense of purpose it did for my parents. I didn't know who I was—not really—and I had no idea who God called me to be. Sensing I needed a direction and needed it fast, I turned to the only thing I thought would fill me with self-worth, self-confidence, and purpose—achievement. But as I'd find years later, though achievement provides a good high in the moment, it doesn't satisfy in the long run. It's like a drug, creating a craving for more, more, more. And one thing is darned sure—success isn't a sufficient life calling. After all, achievement is about what you can do in the moment, but it doesn't speak to who you are past your skin.

The Vine of Faith Calling, the Branches of Vocational Calling

If we Christians are good at anything, it's yammering on about "calling." Growing up, I heard I had a "unique calling," that I ought to find "my calling," and that I should follow God in my "calling." I'm not sure it was explicitly said, but I was led to believe that *calling* and *career* were synonymous, and that the more you honored God, the more you'd achieve in that calling. And because I still attend church, still run in Christian circles, and still listen to sermons from pastors across the country, I continue to hear a lot of messages about the ambiguous concept of *calling*. In fact, as I was writing this chapter, I heard a slick-haired preacher inform his congregation that if you "serve the purpose of the season you're in, you don't have to find your calling; your calling will find you."

31

Huh?

Calling. Calling. Calling. Everyone wants to talk about calling these days. But for the most part, when pastors, priests, rabbis, or motivational gurus talk about calling, it seems they're using it as a code word for a specific thing—your job. Your career. Your vocation. What you do. You've been called to be an engineer (like my dad), or a journalist (like me). You've been called to be an entrepreneur, a teacher, a mother. In my own experience, those notions of calling are focused on what we do in our day-to-day vocations. But that kind of understanding of calling produces unintended consequences. For instance, what happens when you limit the notion of calling to your vocation, your career, or your daily obligations? If you're anything like me, you wrap your *entire identity* up in it. And then? For the sake of your God-given "calling," you'll leverage everything—your time, your talent, your money. You may find yourself losing connection to the things that matter most to you.

If your ultimate calling is to be an engineer, you'll work yourself to the bone trying to climb the ladder, only to find your entire life filled with stress, strain, and lack of peace.

If your ultimate calling is to achieve school success, you'll sacrifice time to get the highest grade possible, only to find that you've missed out on so much life along the way.

If your ultimate calling is to be a journalist, you'll accept every assignment, take every interview, travel to every country, even if it means sacrificing your family, your friends, and your church.

You'll sacrifice things such as your husband, your kids, or your community of faith based on some grandiose notion that God has called you into a particular career. How do I know? I lived it. (Just ask John and my kids.)

Sure, our day-to-day jobs and vocations comprise part of our calling, but we're not so one-dimensional. Just as we're made up of both body and soul, our calling has two distinct facets—a faith or life calling (which I'll term *faith calling* for the sake of simplicity), and a day-to-day work calling (which I'll dub *vocational calling*). As I'll show throughout this book, I've come to realize and firmly believe that those two distinct facets of our callings are interconnected. In fact, it's my belief that everything *we do* (our vocational calling) serves as a vehicle to share *who we are*—people loved by God and called to love God and share his love with the people of this world (our faith calling). And if we're going to live a life of meaning and purpose, we have to make our faith calling our priority.

Faith calling—everyone has one, even if they don't call it that. What is it? For the Christian (or one who believes in God), it is who God has created you to be, and how you've been called to live in response. The atheist or agnostic might view it as the underlying purpose that guides decision-making. Over the years, I've heard various people muse about who we've been created to be (as opposed to what we've been called to do). In my Catholic upbringing, we were taught that mankind was created to know, love, and serve God. The leaders at Morning Star taught that we were to love God and love people. Rabbi Schmuley Boteach, the man known as America's rabbi, whom I interviewed for my podcast *Journeys of Faith with Paula Faris*, said his purpose was to communicate the love of God to people however he could. My friend and longtime co-anchor Dan Harris, who's becoming a bit of an expert on meditation, might say his life purpose is to live a mindful and centered life of compassion, one at peace with the people and world around him. I have an atheist friend who says her life purpose is to love her family, love her neighbor, and be a good person. See? At the end of the day, we all have a sort of guiding principle that defines who we are, who we've been made to *be*. And for

> Everything we do (our vocational calling) serves as a vehicle to share who we are—people loved by God and called to love God and share his love with the people of this world (our faith calling).

33

the most part, we all agree—we've been made to be living examples of compassion and love to others.

As Christians, we draw our faith calling directly from Christ himself. In the book of Matthew, a religious leader asked Jesus what the most important command might be. He answered simply: "'Love the Lord your God with all your heart and with all your soul and with all your mind.' This is the first and greatest commandment. And the second is like it: 'Love your neighbor as yourself'" (Matthew 22:37–39). In other words, the faith calling of the Christian, simply put, is *to love God with everything we have and to love others with the same love God has extended to us*, particularly through Christ. Love God. Love people.

Our faith calling is meant to be solid and directive. *It will never change.* It is meant to connect us to the full life Christ promised when he said, "I am the vine; you are the branches. If you remain in me and I in you, you will bear much fruit" (John 15:5). So in a perfect world, our faith calling informs everything we do and leads to the best, most loving, most God-centered outcomes. But what if we don't root into the vine of our faith calling? We'll become misaligned in our day-to-day lives and prone to be mired in fear, chasing success and always saying yes to the wrong things. We'll tend to grasp the wrong opportunities and sacrifice the things and people we love most. We won't live lives bearing spiritual fruit. At least that was my experience. And doesn't it make sense? After all, Jesus closed his teaching on the vine and the branches with a clear statement: "Apart from me you can do nothing" (John 15:5).

If faith calling speaks to who we are—loved children of God called to share his love with the world—our vocational calling speaks to what we do every day. We may find our vocational calling in any number of fields: journalism, education, business, nonprofit work, parenting, engineering. *But our vocational calling—what we do—can change, whereas our faith calling won't.* Our vocational calling may branch in unforeseen directions, or not. We may climb the corporate ladder, switch industries, or stay at the same desk job for forty years. But no matter which way our vocational calling may or may not branch, our vocations are meant for one purpose—to be a vehicle for sharing God's love with the world.

I was a bona fide believer—God, Jesus his Son, the Holy Spirit, the whole nine yards. Still, I never understood how faith calling and vocational calling operated together, not really. (I thought that *calling* and *career* were synonymous.) And sure, I was a person of faith and didn't hide it from my co-workers, but I didn't allow it to directly influence my decision-making in the office either. I treated my faith calling and my vocational calling as two separate things. Wrapped up in *what I did* (a journalist) instead of *who I was* (loved by God and called to share his love), I was terrified of failure, of not measuring up. So I chased the next achievement, the next bigger story, the next better interview. I said yes to every opportunity, even at the expense of my family and faith, because it gave me a sense of accomplishment and made me feel as if I belonged. The result? My life became unbalanced and unmanageable as I found my identity in vocational success, probably much like my dad in the early days of his engineering career.

I wasn't connected enough with John.

My children constantly wondered aloud when I'd be home. *If* I'd be home.

As things at home became more and more difficult, I began to see that if I kept on that path, my life would become a complete disaster. But as he has a way of doing, God intervened. After a few stubborn attempts to ignore him, I finally paid attention.

Becoming David

I'm not the only one who has missed the connection between their faith calling and vocational calling, of course. Even biblical characters have missed it. Consider David, known as the man after God's own heart. When he was only a shepherd boy, the prophet Samuel anointed him as the future king of Israel. (Talk about a shift in vocational calling.) David didn't ascend to the throne overnight, though. Instead, he returned to the fields, where he continued to protect his father's sheep, practiced slinging stones with his slingshot, and prayed and played songs to God. In the fields, David apparently remained focused on who he was—a humble servant and worshiper of God—as we don't read of him demanding more opportunities, more responsibility, or more privilege. Rooted in his faith calling, David obeyed when God called him to confront the behemoth Goliath with nothing more than a slingshot and the confidence that God would rescue him. We all know the rest of the story. David slew the giant and ultimately became king. Sure, David had particular vocational skills—he was a born leader and a marksman with a slingshot—but his confidence wasn't in his skill, what he could do. His confidence was in his God and in who God made him to be, and David made it known, saying, "The Lord who rescued me from the paw of the lion and the paw of the bear will rescue me from the hand of this Philistine" (1 Samuel 17:37).

Seems like David was pretty rooted in his faith calling, right?

All great men and women, even those who are clear in their faith calling, are prone to lose their way from time to time; David is no exception. Though he honored God as king, though he wrote almost half of the Psalms, though he ultimately became king and tried to rule the people benevolently, David lost sight of his faith calling and became intoxicated by the power of his position, with devastating consequences. Staring down from the royal suite, a high point of the city, he noticed Bathsheba bathing on her roof, and he used his power and influence to have her brought to his room. He enticed her to sleep with him even though she was married to another man, and when it turned out that Bathsheba was pregnant, David ordered her husband, Uriah, to the front lines of battle, a place he was destined to die.

Uriah was killed in battle, and David and Bathsheba's baby died too. By losing sight of his faith calling—to honor, love, and serve God as a humble servant—by relying too much on the power of his vocational calling, the king disconnected from the vine. As a result, he brought pain and devastation to his house, Uriah's house, and the entire nation of Israel. David's great fall still stands as a cautionary tale today.

David's life is an example of what happens when we lose sight of who we are, our underlying purpose, our faith calling. But the truth is, so many of us don't mine the lessons from his story. So many of us are too busy becoming King David, so occupied with chasing what we do that we lose sight of who we are. That's what I did. That's what standout Duke basketball player Jay Williams did as he entered the NBA, but we'll examine that in more detail in chapter 10. An overwhelming number of religious leaders—including Catholic priests and Baptist ministers, just to name two recent examples—lost sight of *who they are*, and as a result, thousands were sexually abused.

Maybe you've never contemplated your faith calling, never defined who you are. Perhaps you've chased success or accomplishment or fitting in without ever asking why.

No matter our religion, we all have a faith calling. And though my faith calling as a Christian was clearly defined by Jesus—love the Lord your God with all your heart, mind, soul, and strength, and love your neighbor as yourself—you might put yours a different way, even if it's as simple as "be a kind, generous, good person." However you define it, know this: Your faith calling describes *who you are*. It should serve as the foundation for everything you do. It should affect the way you interact with people, the way you parent, the way you relate to your spouse, and the way you pursue your vocational calling. Everything should flow from your faith calling.

Maybe you are like I was in high school, in college, and throughout so much of my career, though. Maybe you've never contemplated your faith calling, never defined *who you are*. Perhaps you've chased success or accomplishment or fitting in without ever asking why. If that's you, consider asking yourself:

Do I understand my faith calling, who I am, and my underlying purpose?

Could I write out my faith calling with any sort of clarity?

Do my vocation, my acts of service, my parenting, my side hustle, or my next big idea flow from my faith calling, or is something else steering the ship?

If you have trouble answering these questions, that might be why you carry angst, pressure, and turmoil in your vocation. It might be why you feel as if everyone is getting your leftovers, just as I did. Could it also be why you're willing to take every assignment, chase every opportunity, or compromise your integrity, even to the detriment of those around you? Without understanding who you are, your purpose for living, your faith calling, you won't be able to align who you are with what you do.

The Girl Who Didn't Know Her Faith Calling

Because I never understood the difference between faith calling and vocational calling, I got wrapped up in what I did from the beginning. I set my sights on accomplishment, on perfection.

In high school, my parents offered me a change of scenery, and I jumped on it. I walked into Jackson Baptist High School during my freshman year, ready to prove myself. I was the new girl, didn't know a single soul, and still, the girls welcomed me. They called me Paula instead of Guppy, and they all wore skirts below the knee. There, the students and teachers shared common values, and with the obstacle of fitting in removed, I focused on the things I could control, the things I could achieve.

Like my dad, I was a little insecure, but this wasn't all bad. It was a motivating factor, something that pushed me to do more than I could naturally do. Work hard, keep my nose down, push myself—these became a sort of inner monologue, even if I didn't know it. I poured myself into my studies, and even though I had the worst case of undiagnosed ADD, even though I had to read pages three, four, or five times—often through tears—just to get the information to stick, I graduated with honors. (In fact, I was officially diagnosed with Attention Deficit Disorder during the writing of this book.) I devoted myself to softball and was named all-county. I picked up the clarinet and practiced my way into first chair. I was an accomplishment addict. But no matter how much I succeeded, I was only smart enough for the moment. Good enough for the moment. Worth enough for the moment. I was always left wanting more, so I pushed more. And it was that desire for more that followed me into broadcasting, that kept me chasing bigger markets, bigger opportunities, and higher-profile interviews. But achievement and success in what I did never satisfied me, at least not for long. Come to find out, achievement and success can't sustain a life. But that's a lesson I would not learn for years.

CHAPTER 3

Interview with an International Spy: Clarifying Calling

In my line of work, I have the privilege of interviewing high-profile people at the height of their careers. Politicians, rock stars, actors, and actresses—my interview subjects tend to be public figures, men and women who stand in the cultural limelight. (In fact, during the writing of this book, I interviewed the entire cast of *Avengers: Endgame* for the film's release, and five days later I interviewed the cast of *Star Wars: The Rise of Skywalker.*) It's rare that I'm truly surprised by an interview, especially when the subject is a quieter, flying-under-the-radar sort of person. On rare occasions, though, I meet an unsung luminary.

Someone who has risen to the pinnacle of his career with little public recognition. Someone like David Shedd.

In the weeks following my conversation with James Goldston, I'm a walking bundle of nerves. I've stepped into the unknown, into the breach, and I wonder, *Will this move kill my career?* I don't shake inner voices well, particularly the voice of self-doubt, and in this new season, the voices follow me everywhere.

Who am I apart from my work, my career, my television personality?

What if this new vocational path turns out to be a spectacular failure—in public, no less?

What if I become one of those out-of-sight, out-of-mind television personalities whose best days are behind her?

What would it say about my faith if God doesn't show up when I'm taking such a big risk? Bigger yet, what would it say about me?

At my desk, questions spinning, knowing I have to break the cycle of self-talk, I pick up my phone, scroll through my contacts, and call a longtime friend from Cedarville College (my alma mater), Brent Gibbs. Brent had pursued his vocational calling in the music industry and is well connected with high-profile Christians across industries. He's a trustworthy source, and I figure he'll have a list of compelling names, people of faith who think differently about the ways they express faith in their everyday lives and who might encourage my listeners to do the same.

Brent answers, and we exchange pleasantries. I'm after interview subjects, I tell him, people of faith who are at the top of their games. I can almost hear him nodding along, and he gives me a few names. At the top of that list, he says, is David Shedd.

Who?

Brent describes Shedd as "a government guy" and a man of deep faith. He's a man who knows who he is, and everything he does flows from that understanding, Brent says.

"What does he do?" I asked.

"International intelligence."

"Like, he's a spy?" I push further.

"Maybe. You'll have to ask him."

I'd been in journalism for years, had interviewed so many movers and shakers in the political world, including policy makers, and yet I'd never heard of David Shedd. Brent asks me to trust him, to do my research, and because Brent is an old friend whose word I take at face value, I agree to do just that.

We say our good-byes and hang up our phones, and I turn to my open laptop. In the search bar I type "David Shedd," tap the return key, and wait for the results to populate my screen. Articles and videos pop up. A wiki reference appears on the right side of my screen and with it a short bio: "David R. Shedd is a retired U.S. intelligence officer whose final post was as the acting Director of the Defense Intelligence Agency. He is a former Central Intelligence Agency operative."[1]

Intriguing.

I start plowing through the articles and discover that Shedd is what you might call a big deal in the United States' intelligence community. It doesn't take much reading to discover that he takes his Christian faith seriously too. In fact, it seems to have influenced everything he does. He is the son of second-generation Christian missionaries, and was raised in Bolivia, Chile, Argentina, and Uruguay during a set of particularly volatile years in Latin America. It was those years that shaped both his faith and, ultimately, his vocational calling.

I dig in to his backstory and find that the international spotlight turned to Chile while he was living there in 1970. The United States and the Soviet Union were fighting for influence in the country in the middle of an escalating Cold War, and Chile had just elected avowed Marxist Salvador Allende president, which gave rise to increased tensions in the region. As the news unfolded day by day, a young David Shedd found himself drawn to the news, curious about the relationship between his home country and the country in which he and his parents lived. I read how his passion for international policy was sparked at a young age, how he began to nurse a curiosity in the ways governments dealt with foreign entities, a pretty specific interest for an eleven-year-old boy.

David hadn't been shy about his faith or about how it had influenced his career. Whenever he was interviewed, whenever he spoke, he shared about his Christian home, his Christian education, and his Christian calling. He'd attended Geneva College, a Christian institution in Beaver Falls, Pennsylvania, and though he'd begun as an engineering major, it didn't seem like the right fit. Clear in his faith calling—who he was and what his purpose was in the world—he paid attention to his deepening interest in foreign policy, to

I'd heard of pastors, priests, and rabbis being "called to ministry," but a layman being called into the clandestine services? Not so much.

the ways it seemed to come naturally to him. As he did, he sensed God was moving him into the field of international intelligence.

I'd heard of pastors, priests, and rabbis being "called to ministry," but a layman being called into the clandestine services? Not so much.

After receiving his bachelor of arts degree from Geneva College, Shedd pushed deeper into the direction he felt God was leading him, and he enrolled in Georgetown University, where he received his master's degree from the Edmund A. Walsh School of Foreign Service with an emphasis in Latin American studies. It was a natural fit for Shedd, whose unique upbringing in Latin America made him well suited for his studies. His academic excellence led to other opportunities—more secretive opportunities. From that point forward, he was singularly focused on what he felt was his particular, unique calling.

To call Shedd's résumé impressive would be an insult. He'd risen through the ranks of the intelligence community, starting as an intern in the CIA before becoming a CIA operative. (Was I going to interview a spy?) He'd been posted at embassies in Costa Rica and Mexico from 1984 to 1993. He'd been instrumental in shaping national security policy after 9/11, and had served as the director of National Intelligence before becoming the acting director of the Defense Intelligence Agency (DIA) in 2014, a combat support agency of the Department of Defense.

I was hooked; I couldn't stop reading. Shedd was the perfect example of someone who had climbed to the heights of his chosen vocational career. He'd been called by God, had responded, and now his security clearance was somewhere just below presidential. The things he must know. The secrets.

Maybe I should ask him whether there are aliens at Area 51?

I was scheduled to be in Washington, D.C., to interview Kellyanne Conway, so I asked one of our interview bookers to reach out to Shedd and see if he would sit for an interview. The topic? Faith and calling—particularly, how does a person find him or herself called to international intelligence? Within hours our booker has an answer—Shedd would love nothing more than to give me an hour to discuss faith.

Called to International Espionage

David arrives at the studio in a gray suit and gold tie, somewhat formally dressed as compared with my previous guest, country music star Luke Bryan, who'd worn jeans and a flannel shirt. He smiles, introduces himself with an air of familiarity, and sits across the interview table from me.

The tapes roll and I dig in, sharing a little of Shedd's background with the listeners. I review his unique career path, how he has served for more than thirty years in the intelligence community, under numerous presidents, including George W. Bush and Barack Obama. I turn to Shedd, telling him I want to talk about the role faith plays in the intelligence community, but before we launch into that, there's a question that needs answering.

"Am I technically talking to a spy right now?"

"I think you are."

Hold it together, Paula.

There's a hitch in my breathing, and trying to get a grip, I say, "Oh my gosh, I'm a little nervous."

"Don't be," he says. "We don't have horns or tails."

"No, you don't. But that's why you're a spy, because otherwise it would be a little too obvious, right?"

Well played, Paula.

I press on with the interview, asking him exactly what he believes about the role of faith in vocational life, and for the first time in my life, I hear someone tease out the notions of faith calling and vocational calling, even if he doesn't say it directly:

> I think faith is a central piece of what makes a person. . . . I think every person at the core has a *raison d'être* for life. . . . I see faith central to really shaping who you are by way of your character, your ethics, your way of problem-solving, your view of the world.

Faith underlies and informs our faith calling, Shedd was saying. The way we operate in the world—our character, ethics, problem-solving, *what we do*—flows directly from it. David's faith calling, his *raison d'être* (his reason for life) had been to love God and use his God-given gifts to love and serve the world. And as he stayed connected to that faith calling, as he kept his eyes on it, he began to sense God had a particular vocational calling that flowed from it. But how had he known God was calling him to

To help people discover their calling, Shedd counsels them to pay attention to their natural giftings, their innate curiosities, and the vocational encouragement given by trusted teachers, leaders, and mentors.

a particular career path, especially one as specific as international espionage? (Who knew God needed spies?)

I put it to him straight and ask him how we can know if we've been "called" by God. Does a voice come from the heavens? Did God say to him, "David, I need you to go into the government"?

Smiling, shaking his head, he tells me calling doesn't work that way. In fact, when he counsels young people about discovering their calling, he tells them to pay attention to three things: their natural giftings, their innate curiosities, and the vocational encouragement given by trusted teachers, leaders, and mentors. It was through these three facets—his giftedness in understanding policy, his curiosity in international intelligence, and the encouragement to pursue international relations by his college professors—that Shedd had come to understand God's calling into something very specific.

I break down his template for determining vocational calling in my own terms, forming a mental bullet list, then jot it on my notepad. We find our way to our vocational calling by considering

- our skill sets ("What we're good at," I write);
- what we're curious about ("Curiosities," I write); and
- the skills and proficiencies our friends and mentors recognize in us ("Mentor encouragement," I write).

Minutes before, I'd been doing my best not to lose my cool in front of an international spy. Now I was doing my best not to scream "YES!" and tell him the interview was over. He'd given me a simple formula for examining my own vocational calling, for determining whether my current path, odd as it was, was a right path for me. He'd given me the tools I needed to understand how my career was unfolding.

The interview ends and I wonder, *Why haven't I heard this kind of super-granular way of determining God's vocational calling for my life?* Why had the notion of calling been so ambiguous to me for all these years? Why did it take a spy to articulate what vocational calling looked and sounded like?

Finding Vocational Calling

During the writing of this book, I attended a Christian conference, the pump-you-up kind with lights, Coldplay-style worship music, and a large stage with big-name Christian speakers and preachers. Speaker after speaker took the stage and talked about calling. They asked what we were called to do and whether we were living into our calling. They tossed the phrase around casually, as if we all understood what the word *calling* meant, what ours was, and how we might pursue it. One preacher said it so many times, I could have turned it into a drinking game. (If you'd have thrown one back every time he said the word *calling*, you'd be pass-out drunk in ten minutes.)

Not once did any of those speakers give us the tools to understand what calling was, how to discover our unique calling, or the connection between faith and calling. They didn't explain how each of us has a faith calling (a *raison d'être*, as Shedd put it) that shapes everything. They didn't show how *what we do* (our vocational calling) flows directly from *who we are* (our faith calling), nor did they expound upon the dangers of conflating *calling* with *career*. No practical tools were given to the audience regarding how to participate with God in pursuing our day-to-day work.

I sat in that auditorium listening to those preachers, and as I reflected on my time with David, I began to understand just how nuanced our callings are. How unique. How special. After all, no two people have identical predispositions, innate curiosities, and the same set of trusted leaders speaking into them. Each of us is called to walk into our vocational calling in the way only we can.

Consider two biblical examples. Peter and his brother Andrew were Galilean fishermen, and both had been called to follow Jesus as "fishers of men" (Matthew 4:19 ESV). This sounds like the perfect alignment of faith calling and vocational calling, if you ask me. Despite their similarities, their predispositions and giftings were different. Peter was more headstrong, more brash, what we might call a "born leader" in today's vernacular. Andrew, on the other hand, seemed to be quieter, less obtrusive, and he was always bringing people to Jesus. He brought Peter to Jesus (John 1:41–42), as well as a little boy with loaves and fish (John 6:8–9), and went to Jesus on behalf of a group of Greeks who wanted to meet him (John 12:20–22).

Peter and Andrew were gifted uniquely, and while called to the same life purpose—to lead people to Christ—they took different vocational routes. After his death, burial, and resurrection, Jesus called Peter to lead the early church (talk about being spoken into by a trusted mentor), and church tradition says Andrew became a missionary in the region of the Black Sea.

Two brothers. Each called by Jesus. Each with some of the same vocational gifts (fishing). But their predispositions, their unique curiosities, and the different assignments given by their trusted rabbi landed them in different, even if somewhat similar, vocational callings. They were both Christian leaders of the early church. But within that broad category of vocation calling to ministry, their individual expressions of vocation were nuanced, unique. And under their unique vocational callings was a common faith calling—to love the Lord with everything they had, and to use their lives to share God's love with the world.

You may have the same faith calling as others in your chosen vocation. (I'm not the only Christian in broadcast journalism, for instance.) You might even have the same general vocational aims (just as Peter, Andrew, Paul, and Ananias had the vocational aims of sharing the Christian faith). But because you have different skills and gifts, different curiosities, and because different people have spoken into your life (which is to say nothing of the differences in your life experiences), your vocational calling is unique to you. Just as David Shedd's unique gifts (a mind for policy), curiosities (interests in both Latin America and international relations), and mentors (the voices of his parents, professors, and later his bosses) set this course of his unique vocational calling, so will yours. And whether you're in broadcast journalism, international espionage, or are a stay-at-home parent, the way you pursue your vocational calling will be unlike anyone else's. It will be as unique as the code of your DNA, as unique as your fingerprint, as unique as your ear print.

Your ear print? (Can you hear me now?)

Calling—the Shape of an Ear Print

Richard Gray wrote about the individuality of the human ear in a 2017 BBC article, "The Seven Ways You Are Totally Unique." According to Gray, the "complex patterns of ridges and furrows formed by the cartilage of your outer ears are remarkably unique to you." Gray continued,

> This has led to 3D scanning techniques that build up a detailed model of the ear and new methods that extract distinctive geometric features of the ear. By analysing a combination of features, such as the distance from the lobe to two points on the upper edge, it is possible to recognize someone from even a fuzzy picture of their ear with 99.6% accuracy in just 0.02 milliseconds.[2]

As if this isn't enough, the unique shape of our ears, combined with the microscopic hair cells in the cochlea, affects our hearing, meaning that each of us interprets the sounds of the world around us a little differently. And now scientists believe that all those tiny variations in the shape and structures of our ears make it possible to unlock your phone or smart device simply by lifting it to your ear. Some believe that your ear may soon become the easiest way to identify you. (Let me ask again: Can you hear me now?)

As complex and unique as our ears may be, our lives are far more complex, far more unique. We're shaped and formed in unique ways by different gifts, curiosities, and life experiences. And those life experiences give us different ways of hearing, different ways of understanding both our faith calling—*who we are and who we've been called to be*—and the vocational calling—*what we've been called to do*—that flows from it. As a result, we all have unique ways of living out our vocational callings, ways that might not fit with the run-of-the-mill practices of our respective industries. We might be called to open our imaginations, to ask what it looks like to bring what we do more in line with who we are, even if that means leaving the normal career path to pursue something scary or ambiguous, such as a faith podcast. But before we can take those steps, don't we need to be well acquainted with our faith calling? And shouldn't we examine our current life situation to ensure our vocation flows from that faith calling, that it flows from who we are? Shouldn't we also make sure we're pressing into the vocational callings God has placed on our lives?

Maybe you're like I was before the David Shedd interview. Maybe you've never stopped to examine your life, to see whether you were following your vocational calling. Maybe you never considered whether your current vocation flows from your predispositions, your curiosities, and the encouragement of trusted people who could see the dream for you before you could see it for yourself. Maybe you stumbled into a job because it seemed like the next right move, and after all, you had to do *something*. Worse yet, maybe you avoided a true vocational calling because you were afraid of the risk, afraid of the nature of the work, afraid of the failure. If you fall into the last category, it's okay. I was that girl for a very long season.

As important as it is to identify, know, and internalize your faith calling, it is just as important to identify, know, and internalize your vocational calling. And if you've gotten off track, if you can't quite say what your vocational calling is, do a little digging. Ask the questions Shedd asked:

- What are my innate skills?
- What am I curious about?
- What skills and proficiencies have my mentors and friends recognized in me?

Then ask,

- Is there anything getting in the way of that calling, anything such as fear?

That's what I did after the podcast interview.

In the weeks following the interview, I played Shedd's words about calling on repeat. Why had I been so scared in this new and exciting season of my life? Why had I been so afraid I'd lose my identity without the weekend anchor desk, without my heavy on-air load? Why was this fear of the loss of identity limiting my imagination for what was possible, for a thriving podcast, for more in-depth stories about faith in the workplace, for *who knows what?* Was I afraid the unique direction of my career wouldn't work out, that I'd be labeled washed-up, or irrelevant, or a failure because I hadn't followed the standard industry path? Probably. But as I reflected on David's vocational calling formula, I began to see how I'd been moving into the sweet spot of my vocational calling, even if I didn't exactly know it.

> **As important as it is to identify, know, and internalize your faith calling, it is just as important to identify, know, and internalize your vocational calling.**

Hadn't I been a questioner from the earliest age, an interviewer, a challenger who wouldn't take no for an answer?

52

Wasn't I innately curious about everything?

And hadn't others encouraged me to explore broadcasting along the way?

I could see it now: I'd been called to a career in broadcast journalism. And though there was still fear, still a lack of clarity about my path forward, I couldn't let that fear disrupt my vocational calling, especially now that I had such clarity. I couldn't let the fear keep me from living my faith calling out through that vocation, even though I wasn't exactly sure what that meant, yet. Looking back, I had almost let fear disrupt both my faith and my vocation once before. I wouldn't let it happen again.

CHAPTER 4

The Calling Bigger than My Fear

There are many things I wish I had known in my high school days, in college, and early on in my career. I wish I had known who I was apart from what I did or accomplished or the accolades I received. And I wish I had understood that finding purpose, meaning, or identity in my success was a no-win situation. If I had been rooted in my faith calling, if I had allowed the things I did to flow from that, if I hadn't allowed myself to be defined by my performance, maybe I wouldn't have floundered in fear for so many years. But I didn't know, and that's not my story. My story was one of fear.

From the beginning, I was a girl marked by fear. The regular childhood fears many share—fear of the dark, of spiders, of heights, of creepy dolls or balloon-carrying clowns? Sure. (Truth be told, I'm still scared of the dark and heights and creepy clowns.) Those fears, however, were nothing compared with the less concrete, less identifiable, more existential fear. My deepest fear—a common fear among many—was the fear of failure, and it paralyzed me from my earliest years. The fear followed me to high school and plagued me until I discovered the temporary fix for my nagging lack of confidence, a kind of drug cocktail I used to numb that fear. Accomplishment. Achievement. Success. These were my drugs of choice. They still are. And Jackson Baptist High School was my first drug pusher.

At JBHS I poured myself into my studies, into band, into whatever job I could hustle, into whatever might bring the high of accomplishment. When I scored an A in any class—*high*. When a teacher complimented me—*high*. When I was named first chair clarinet in the regional band—*so high*. Through success and achievement, I found a place, an identity, a sense of self-worth. I was *Paula the Good Student*, *Paula the Musician*, and *Paula the Overachiever*. And though it wasn't conscious, a subtle belief began to creep in: I was only as good as my next accomplishment, my next achievement, the next rung of the ladder I climbed. I was as good as the next thing I did.

> **When the high of achievement wore off, that fear of failure came screaming back, more debilitating, crippling, and paralyzing than before.**

Here's the truth about achievement—it's no different from any other drug. You need more and more to keep you rolling, and if you don't get it, you experience a certain sort of withdrawal. When the high of achievement wore off, that fear of failure came screaming back, more debilitating, crippling, and paralyzing than before. And so I chased more success, more achievement, doubled my efforts in my studies, in band, in softball. Still, the voice of self-doubt whispered. What if I plateaued? What if the next thing I did—the next test, concert, or game—turned out to be an utter failure, a total dumpster fire? What would that say about me? Wouldn't it diminish me? Wouldn't it make me a little less valuable?

That voice of fear was a constant tormentor, and I'd do anything to silence it. So if something wasn't a natural fit, if it would lead to inevitable failure, I'd give up and walk away in an effort to silence the voices of potential failure.

Soccer—I quit.

Gymnastics—quit.

Basketball, volleyball—I didn't even try for fear of failure.

And though I thought quitting might silence the inner monologue of self-doubt, it didn't. It just confirmed what I already knew: I was a failure. See the double-edged sword? Sticking with anything that might lead to failure wasn't an option, but quitting only reinforced the old narratives. I wasn't strong enough, good enough, worth enough. And that's when I heard the song playing over and over in my head.

Guppy, guppy, you're the one . . .

Still, my time at Jackson Baptist High School was more up than down, more success than failure. Because it was a smaller school, I could try new things with some certainty of at least limited success, even things I wasn't sure were in my strike zone, like drama and theater. I enrolled in Mr. Barsuhn's drama class, in part because he was such a beloved teacher. (Truth be told, at such a small school, there weren't many other elective options.) Still struggling with self-confidence, I didn't try out for lead roles. Instead, I hoped to maintain a more behind-the-scenes presence, bit parts. Mr. Barsuhn saw through me though. He wouldn't have it.

"Paula, you're the narrator in *Tilly*."

"But that has a lot of lines," I protested.

"I know. You can do it," he responded with a smile. He was so sure. I wasn't.

He handed me the script; I was afraid of letting him down, so I dove in and memorized my lines. As I did, I was surprised to find I didn't hate it. In fact, I almost enjoyed performing in front of a crowd on opening night. As I walked from the gym-turned-theater that evening, the high of accomplishment washed over me. No, I wasn't a born actor, but narrating the story was a fit, something that felt like second nature. So when it came time for the next play, I was cast as the narrator again. And to my surprise, I had even more fun.

Toward the end of my junior year, Mr. Barsuhn encouraged me. He told me I had a gift for storytelling and said I should use it in my career. How? "Have you considered broadcast journalism?" he asked. I hadn't, I told him, but it made so much sense. After all, what are news anchors and reporters but storytellers?

Wouldn't it be fun to tell stories for a living?

I don't hate the thought.

As graduation approached and my days at JBHS were coming to a close, I knew I had a decision to make. Where would I attend college and what would I study? (These were the days before it was socially acceptable to take a gap year to "find yourself" in Paris.) For as long as I could remember, I'd dreamed of standing in Michigan Stadium, wearing maize and blue, and rooting for my Wolverines in the student section. My dad passed down his love for Michigan football; it was treated with an almost religious reverence in my house. Bo Schembechler (who is still the most memorable interview of my career) was an icon in our home, and Jim Harbaugh was my first imaginary boyfriend (and yes, I'm embarrassed I just admitted that). But though the University of Michigan seemed the obvious choice and was only thirty minutes from home, my dad wasn't so sure. I was still a bit of a follower, he said, and he worried I might get lost on such a large campus. Had I considered any smaller schools, Christian schools, schools a little farther from home?

I hadn't really, though there was one school I had visited the previous year. Cedarville College, a Christian liberal arts college in Ohio, hosted a band symposium I had attended, clarinet devotee that I was. It was a conservative, Bible-based college, and it promoted its economic value, though it would still cost an arm and a leg to earn a degree there. Its smaller class sizes were a selling point, and with only 3,500 students and a beautiful campus that stretched over one hundred acres, there seemed to be space to breathe. You could know almost everyone by name and still get anywhere on campus by foot. No alcohol was allowed, and there was a strict dress code as well as daily chapel. Students weren't allowed to watch movies at the local movie theater. (A rule that changed after my freshman year.) It was the University of Michigan's exact opposite, and it seemed like the sort of place I might find a fit. Dad agreed. I enrolled. And that was that.

I arrived at Cedarville in the fall of 1993, and strolled into my advisor's office to declare a major. With a knack for telling stories, an innate curiosity that fueled my incessant question asking, and the encouragement of Mr. Barsuhn, I chose communications, which would include studies in broadcasting and journalism. It was a field of study that fit squarely within my gifts, one in which I knew I could succeed even if the idea of freezing on camera, of missing lines, of failing in a public forum was daunting. And besides, I didn't plan on stepping in front of the camera anyway. I could put my knack for storytelling to use in other ways: producing, editing, writing, and the like. I put my head down and went to work, chasing another hit of success.

I was the kind of student who put in the hours, burned the midnight oil. I worked to impress the teachers, and especially wanted to make a good impression on my two favorite broadcasting and communications professors, Mr. Leightenheimer and Mr. Kragel. But when they offered me reporting roles in class, I declined. I opted for other roles if I could, roles in the production room, behind the camera, behind the scenes. There, my screw-ups would be more hidden. My failures wouldn't be as public. (And besides, while behind the camera filming men's basketball, I could keep a close eye on John Krueger, a basketball All-American at Cedarville.)

Mr. L and Mr. K kept pushing, telling me I needed to be open to the possibility of being on air, that I needed to pursue it. After class, Mr. K asked me to wait around, and when the last of the students had trickled out, he said, "Paula, I'd like you to consider getting in front of the camera." My stomach turned the minute he said it, and my fingers tingled. I didn't respond, so he continued. "Try it. See if you like it, if you're any good at it. You don't want to look back on your life and wonder, 'Would I have been good at reporting? I guess I'll never know.'"

Mr. K was right, of course, but I couldn't see myself on air. So I shied away from the spotlight, hid any aspirations of being good enough to be in front of the camera. There were others who were more polished, prettier, better equipped to be the lead anchors or journalists.

During my freshman year, Mr. K announced he would be leading a group of students interested in broadcast journalism to participate in a Summer Olympics Broadcasting Program. We would put in two years of training, and if we completed it, we'd have the opportunity to work with the network crews during the 1996 summer games in Atlanta. I jumped on the opportunity along with ten other Cedarville students, and when the summer of 1996 rolled around, we all made the cut. I was heading to Atlanta.

I could choose the crew I'd shadow and work with at the games, so I picked one on the production side. Working on the Electronic News Gathering team, I watched the magnificent seven (Shannon Miller, Dominique Moceanu, Dominique Dawes, Kerri Strug, Amy Chow, Amanda Borden, and Jaycie Phelps) in the practice rounds of women's gymnastics. I attended equestrian and cycling events, and even met Arnold Schwarzenegger. But no matter where I was, I kept a close eye on the reporters, holding microphones and delivering updates on-air.

As I did, I nursed a secret ambition. I wanted to be the one holding the microphone, delivering the news. I wanted to be on-air.

Why couldn't I bring myself to try?

Why was I so afraid of failing?

What did I have to lose?

Opportunities lead to opportunities, especially when you're a performance-driven achiever chasing a hit of anything that will boost your self-esteem. So what had begun as a sort of internship for the summer Olympics turned into a spring internship in Atlanta for CNN Sports Illustrated in 1997. While in Atlanta, I spent time with the anchors, heavy hitters like Chris Rose and Daryn Kagan. I watched them deliver the sports, wanting to have the courage and confidence it took to get in front of the camera. Still, the question nagged: Was I good enough to do *that*?

I nursed a secret ambition. I wanted to be the one holding the microphone, delivering the news. I wanted to be on-air.

I wasn't. I knew it. So I didn't try. Even though the earliest signs of vocational calling were present— the gifts, the curiosity, the encouragement of others— without the confidence that comes from being rooted in my faith calling, without knowing who I was, I became afraid of what I'd been called to do. In that fear, I became no better than Jonah, the biblical prophet. I fled from my vocational calling.

My college years drew to a close, and I was at a loss. I'd met a boy at Cedarville, that lanky basketball standout John Krueger, and we'd started dating. It was going somewhere, I thought, and staying in the area was a priority. But though I'd earned a degree in broadcasting and communications, I didn't apply for the right kinds of jobs at the news affiliates in Columbus or the surrounding area. Instead, I did something more rational. I worked three jobs with little connection to my degree. (Oh, the things a lack of self-confidence will make us do.)

During the day, I worked at Mills James, a video production company in Columbus that specialized in marketing and promotional materials. It was grunt work, but I told myself it would keep me close to John as I tended to the mundane tasks of coordinating edits, scheduling shoots, and cataloguing the equipment out in the field. It was an entry-level position, an hourly slog that didn't cover rent, nor would it make a dent in the mountain of student debt I'd incurred at Cedarville. To make ends meet, I took a part-time job at Arby's stacking roast beef sandwiches, and I cleaned apartments on the weekends.

Organize production crews, stack sandwiches, clean the toilets—it was a rhythm I couldn't sustain, so I turned in my apron at Arby's and started looking for something more lucrative.

The thought nagged that maybe I should give TV reporting a go. But would that mean I'd have to leave Columbus? Could John and I make it long-distance? More than any of that, was I even worth hiring? Was I good enough to make a career in broadcast journalism? I didn't know, but I didn't try either. So I focused on paying my bills instead. I received a phone call from the hiring coordinator at WSNY-FM Sunny 95, informing me that he'd been impressed with my academic record, my résumé, and the brief interview I'd given a few weeks before, and that they had a sales job if I wanted it. I jumped. The money was better than I had imagined, and I could work remotely. It was 1999. By the end of the year, I would be slinging radio spots.

Fear of Old Testament Proportions

The fear of failure—don't so many of us struggle with it? We know people by their successes—by what they do and how well they do it. One of the first questions you ask someone is, "What do you do for a living?" He's a phenomenal surgeon. She's an award-winning author. They're a musical power couple. (Yes, I love Beyoncé and Jay-Z as much as the next girl.) And if success is the currency of our day, the thing that defines us, wouldn't failure do the same? If you're anything like me, afraid of being defined by your failures, wouldn't you do anything to avoid that feeling?

If you answered yes, you're in good company.

The Old Testament prophet Jonah was given a particular vocational calling: "The word of the Lord came to Jonah son of Amittai: 'Go to the great city of Nineveh and preach against it, because its wickedness has come up before me'" (Jonah 1:1–2). There was *no way* to confuse the message. God called a particular person to a particular place to do a particular thing. But although Jonah heard God's voice, he exercised his legs and ran from his vocational calling.

If you have darkened the doors of a church, synagogue, or mosque, I'll bet you know the story. Jonah hopped a boat for Tarshish, a town that some believe was more than 2,500 miles away—essentially the distance from Los Angeles to New York—in the opposite direction of the Gentile town of Nineveh. Why? The text doesn't say directly, but I asked my friend and "America's Rabbi" Shmuley Boteach, who said, "[Jonah] feared if the Gentiles heeded God's call for repentance, he would make the sinful Jews look bad." There it was—*fear*. And although this wasn't the same sort of fear of failure I'd struggled with, it's still instructive. Jonah's fear led him by the lip. It impacted him and others.

The biblical text records, "Then the Lord sent a great wind on the sea, and such a violent storm arose that the ship threatened to break up. All the sailors were afraid, and each cried out to his own god. And they threw the cargo into the sea to lighten the ship" (Jonah 1:4–5). You might recall the rest of the story. Jonah outed his disobedience—a disobedience born in fear—and he suggested that the men shouldn't throw the cargo overboard. They should throw *him* overboard, he said, thinking God might spare the sailors if he was not on the ship. (Which begs this question: Why was Jonah less afraid of being tossed into the stormy sea than he was of going to preach to a Gentile horde?)

Ultimately, Jonah was pitched into the sea, and he was swallowed by the great fish. But then God directed that fish to make his way to Nineveh, where Jonah was "discarded" on the beach. (Let's not imagine what that might have looked like.) Talk about God directing your calling! And so, the man who'd been too afraid had been given a second opportunity.

See how Jonah was plagued by fear, and how it disrupted his faith calling? Jonah's fear is the plague of being human. And those same fears still plague us today. All of us. Even the most successful among us.

Overcoming fear by knowing who we are

In chapter 2 we explored and defined our faith calling and vocational calling. In chapter 3 we learned how to identify our potential vocational calling, and how to examine whether we are in our sweet spot. If you've lost sight of your faith calling or if you haven't pursued your vocational calling, ask yourself why. Is it possible that you've allowed fear to take root, to choke out your faith calling and disrupt your vocational calling?

> **If you've lost sight of your faith calling or if you haven't pursued your vocational calling, ask yourself why. Is it possible that you've allowed fear to take root?**

As we push further into understanding both our faith callings and vocational callings and how fear might disrupt either, ask yourself these questions:

> *What is preventing me from walking into my vocational calling? Is it the fear of failure, the fear of being too old to make a career shift, the fear of being too unskilled?*
>
> *What's the worst thing that could happen if I fail while pursuing my vocational calling?*

If I know my faith calling—who I am—does failure in my vocational
calling even matter? (Because it's not so much about what you
do as who you're doing it for, right?)

How would knowing my faith calling give me confidence as I pursue
my vocational calling?

Fear is a liar, a dream-slayer. Fear will end your vocation before it
even begins. Fear can short-circuit God's best for you if you let it.
Fear—it must be rooted out, even if it requires an audacious step.

One Small Step Past Fear, One Giant Leap into Broadcasting

It was a September morning in 2001, and by all measures, I'd achieved
success on the job. I'd been named Rookie of the Year at Sunny 95, and
though it wasn't a fulfilling career, the money was good, and newlywed
as John and I were, that didn't hurt.

John had left our apartment hours before and was already in his
office at Central State University, a historically black college where he
was a newly minted basketball coach. I was working out in the apartment gym, and as I took a swig from my water bottle, I looked at the
television, tuned to NBC. Something was off. Matt Lauer and Katie
Couric were hosting *The Today Show* that morning, but their familiar
faces were not on the screen. Instead, a smoke-consumed World Trade
Center filled the frame of the television.

Stepping off the treadmill, I turned up the volume and listened
as the morning anchors of *Today* kept calm tones as they spoke with
eyewitnesses and journalists on the ground, who were watching the
buildings burn in lower Manhattan. A plane had hit the building, the
woman on the other end of the line said, and while she was talking,
another plane slammed right into the second World Trade tower.

What is happening?!

I bolted from the gym and ran to our apartment to watch the coverage. I leaned forward on the edge of couch. There was a third hijacked plane, it was reported, and it had been flown into the Pentagon. My fingers were tingling, my body numb. Was I breathing? Should I call John? I didn't reach for the phone, though. Instead, I kept watching.

The news unfolded as if in slow motion. The tower that had been hit second fell, followed shortly by the tower that had been hit first. I listened as the broadcasters interviewed person after person, somehow keeping their cool as they did their jobs. I watched images of the smoking Pentagon. I listened as the stories unfolded—the breaking numbers of injuries and fatalities, the grounding of all American air traffic, the shutdown of the financial markets, the speculation of who the terrorists were behind the attacks.

For the rest of the day, I flipped through the channels and watched the reporters deliver the news. The legendary Peter Jennings on ABC. Dan Rather on CBS. They were focused, working with others to tell the most important story of their reporting careers. This was what they'd been trained to do, and as I watched them deliver the breaking news over the footage of a burning lower Manhattan, I had an epiphany.

In fear, I had run from the very thing I was meant to do. It was time to stop running.

In that moment, I knew Mr. Barsuhn, Mr. L, and Mr. K had seen the dream for me before I had seen it for myself. They had encouraged me to pursue a career in journalism, but I had avoided it, afraid I wasn't capable enough, good enough, or worthy of that kind of career. I'd been too afraid of failing, of letting them down. But now my resolve was bigger than my fear, and I knew it was time to quit my job selling radio spots. It was time to let go of the money, push through the fear, and pursue something more important. But even as I wondered whether I was crazy for wanting to pursue this new direction, a Scripture came to mind. It was a word given to Joshua before he was commissioned to occupy the Promised Land: "As I was with Moses, so I will be with you" (Joshua 3:7 ESV). In that moment, I knew: When God calls you, he'll equip you.

John came home early and sat with me on the couch as we watched the coverage into the evening. That night, I mustered up the courage to out my dream, to tell John I wanted to pursue a job in broadcasting. When I did, he just nodded and agreed it was time for me to make a move. I had finally decided to push past the fear. I'd decided to accept my vocational calling. I went in to work that Friday and gave my two weeks' notice.

CHAPTER 5

How to Cultivate a Desire Bigger than Any Fear

I had a clear vocational path and a promise to hold on to. But that didn't mean I wasn't scared. Two decades' worth of insecurities don't evaporate overnight. But for the first time in earnest, I'd decided to pursue a dream, even if I didn't know where to start, much less whether I could succeed in the industry. So I pulled my résumé together, which had only my college journalism experience, and set out to find any job in broadcasting.

I limited my initial job search to Dayton, Ohio, because after I quit my job, John had become the primary breadwinner overnight, and we needed to stay close to Central State where he was coaching, so he could pull down the big bucks. Which is to say barely enough to cover our rent and grocery bills. I went to every news station in town, which didn't take long because there were only a handful, and I submitted my résumé to disinterested human resource managers. I'd do anything, I told whomever would listen. I'd start in the mailroom if I had to. I knew I just needed to get my foot in the door and I'd be able to work my way up. Was my confidence unfounded? Sure. But I didn't know any better.

Weeks passed without any luck. Then, after a day of substitute teaching (a girl's gotta make *some* money), I returned to my apartment on a brisk October afternoon to a blinking light on my answering machine. I pressed play, listening as the hiring coordinator at WKEF/WRGT, the Fox and NBC dual affiliate in Dayton, asked me to call her back. They'd seen my résumé, she said, and they wanted to schedule an interview. I scribbled the number, picked up the phone, and dialed.

The phone rang for what seemed like an eternity before the hiring coordinator answered. I gave her my name and told her I was calling in response to her message.

"What is the position?" I asked.

"Production assistant. It pays minimum wage but it's a good starting place," she said.

I agree to take the interview, and we set a time for the following day.

When I pulled into the parking lot of the two-tone beige building with the call sign plastered in large letters on the side and a massive broadcasting tower that appeared to be jutting out of the roof, my stomach turned, and the questions and fear set in. How assertive should I be, how straightforward? My résumé wasn't shabby for someone who'd only been out of college for four years, but I had no on-air experience listed. Should I tell the interviewer I hoped to work my way up? Should I tell him I intended to be on air?

I'd like to tell you I felt powerful, even invincible, as I walked into the studio for my interview. I'd like to tell you I was firm in my vocational calling and knew God would equip me for the interview. The truth is, I'm not sure how I didn't wobble out of my heels as I followed the receptionist to Ian Rubin's office.

"I'm Ian, the news director at the station," he said, stretching his hand across the table. I gave him the firmest handshake I could, hoping he wouldn't notice how sweaty my palm was. He smiled, gesturing to a chair across the table, and I sat. After exchanging a few pleasantries, he asked about my experience at Cedarville, then about my career in radio sales. He wondered why I'd leave a lucrative job to pursue a minimum-wage production assistant job, one in which I'd be a glorified gofer.

"I'd eventually like to report," I said, playing all my cards. "I'm just trying to get my foot in the door."

Rubin didn't have to tell me that it probably wouldn't happen in Dayton, a relatively large TV market. I knew the realities of the business. Dayton was the sixty-fourth largest news market in the country (out of 210). This was not the kind of place where news reporters cut their teeth. If I wanted to begin a career in broadcasting, if I wanted to make it on air, I'd need to move to Missoula, Montana; or North Platte, Nebraska; or Juneau, Alaska. I'd need to start in these smaller (and much colder) markets and work my way up.

"I understand that probably won't happen here," I said, "but it's my goal. I want to report."

Very formal. Very professional. Was I projecting confidence?

"I hear you," he said, then offered me the job as a glorified gofer and asked when I could start. Immediately, I told him, and no more than a week later, I was in the studio.

The production team didn't ease me into the job. They positioned me at the edge of the deep end of the pool without bothering to ask whether I could swim, then gave me a shove. I took to it, though, and learned by doing. I ran teleprompters (which I had some familiarity with through my degree at Cedarville), dispatched news crews, assisted with any needs that came up during broadcasting, and helped write stories. I moved from experience to experience, always on the edge of another growth curve, always wondering when I'd fail profoundly in front of the team. It didn't take long.

As the lowest crew member on the totem pole, I became the target for a fair amount of hazing. It came with the territory, I figured, and most of it was in good fun, but there were moments when the hazing escalated to something on par with castigation. Months into my new job, I'd written a script for a news story (about what, I can't recall). After reading it, our lead female anchor stood in the middle of the newsroom and yelled, "You buried the lead! That's journalism 101!"

Now, for those of you who never took Journalism 101, allow me to explain. "Burying the lead" refers to minimizing the most important part of a story in the headline. For instance, if a factory fire in Detroit killed twenty-five people, a proper headline would read "Twenty-Five Die in Detroit Factory Fire," instead of "Factory Fire in Detroit, Fatalities Reported." It's not a complicated concept for those who've

Maybe I wasn't a natural, but quitting wasn't an option. God had called me, and he would equip me.

been in and around journalism, and I stood there wondering, *Had I committed the unpardonable journalistic sin?* As I considered it, an iciness settled over the studio. All eyes were on me, and with them the crushing weight of my own failure.

I slinked back to my workstation, ears burning. Maybe I wasn't a natural, but quitting wasn't an option. God had called me, and he would equip me. As I remembered his promise, something like resolve settled in my stomach.

I will be on the air.

No one—not even the lead anchor at the station—can disrupt my career.

I'll work twice as hard to earn back their trust.

And just like that, what would have led me to quit years earlier, now propelled me to try harder.

A few weeks passed, and I considered how I could develop my skills. More, I considered how I could create some kind of opportunity. I had developed a relationship with the crew in the sports department, and one day while talking with one of the anchors, Ryan Brant, I had an idea.

"On my downtime, would it be okay if I borrowed the department's camera equipment?"

"Why?" he asked.

"I'd like to make a tape of myself doing some interviews, maybe a stand-up in the field."

"Why?" he asked again, smiling. And that's when I told him exactly what I'd told Ian: "I want to be a reporter one day."

He didn't call me crazy. In fact, he smiled, encouraged me, and said he'd do whatever he could to help. "But," he said, "you can only borrow the equipment during downtime, when the sports department won't need it."

Score.

For months I borrowed the gear on the sly. I'd pack a forty-pound camera, a forty-pound camera pack, and a heavy tripod into the back of the news van and find local sporting events. I made my way to a few Dayton University basketball games, shot some footage, and recorded an interview or two. I shot a few standups (the industry term for a field report), which required a great deal of choreography as I positioned myself in front of the camera, recorded test footage, checked my framing, then repositioned myself in the same spot for the full report. Once, I packed the gear in the news van and made my way to the ballfields to cover our local minor league baseball team, the Dayton Dragons. There, I lugged the camera, battery pack, and tripod onto the roof of an adjacent building and shot game footage. I made my way back to the stadium, grabbed my interviews, finished my standup, and returned to the studio.

I edited all those pieces and compiled an audition tape, which is sort of a reporter's résumé. Still a production assistant, not knowing whether I could hack it in broadcast journalism, I asked Ian whether he'd take a look at the tape. Knowing I'd never start a reporting career in Dayton, I just wanted his feedback. And humiliating as it could have been, he popped the video in on the spot and watched it right in front of me. I waited for his response. Held my breath.

"Not bad," he said. "Why don't you make another tape."

There it was—a crack, a sliver of hope. And I intended to make the most of it.

I set out to make another tape, one-man-banding it (the term journalists use for shooting, editing, and producing by yourself) around the Dayton area. But before I could even produce a second tape, the crack became a wide-open door. As I was sitting in the newsroom and working on an upcoming newscast, Ian strolled in and tapped me on the shoulder. Leaning down, so only the two of us could hear, he said, "I'm going to put you on the air." I turned, looked over my shoulder to see if it was some kind of joke, some hazing ritual, but Ian had already turned and was heading to the door. I'd done it. I'd earned my spot.

I'd start in the field by covering a few human-interest stories for the news desk, then I'd move to the sports department. I'd keep shooting, editing, and producing my own segments, and I'd anchor at the sports desk from time to time. And despite the fact that this represented a significant promotion, I wouldn't receive any sort of pay raise. Also, I'd still keep up with my production assistant duties.

"You'll anchor one day, run the teleprompter the next. Will that work?" Ian asked.

Would it ever.

I poured myself into the job, attacking it with the overzealous ferocity of any young twentysomething—an overzealousness that wasn't particularly appreciated. Almost as soon as I began reporting, one male co-worker said women didn't belong in sports broadcasting. In fact, he said I would never make it in sports broadcasting unless I showed my breasts. From then on, he sabotaged me, running the wrong tapes on-air in an effort to get in my head, to intimidate me. Could I handle this, the pressure of working in such a male-dominated world?

I could have shared these things with management and they would have taken care of it, but I chose not to raise a stink. I wouldn't let the pressure, intimidation, or the fear drive me to quit. I wouldn't let one small-minded man keep me from succeeding. Clear in my vocational calling, I doubled my efforts.

I'll show them all.

Between my on-air segments, I kept up with all my other production assistant tasks. I ran the prompters, wrote for the shows, helped with editing. Thirty minutes before my segments, I'd hustle to the dressing room to do my own hair and makeup. After the segment, I'd go out to the field to shoot a story or stay late to edit film. I didn't know how I'd ever make it to the bigger stage or what my next steps would be, but I trusted what I'd heard from God in those hours after 9/11. If struggle was what it took to accomplish his purpose, to succeed, I'd be glad to struggle. And as I set my sights on God's vocational calling on my life, the criticism, the intimidation, and the sabotaging became less frightening. Clear in my vocational calling, I was confident I could push through whatever challenge they threw at me.

Fear: An Internal Reality from External Circumstances

Fear is an internal reality, that much is true. But it doesn't always come from your own voices of self-doubt. Sometimes, fear is stoked by external circumstances, by those who tell you you're not good enough, or smart enough, or capable enough, or even that you're just not in the right place at the right time. Sometimes, fear is fueled by harassment (sexual or otherwise) or sabotage. How do we face those external circumstances without letting fear get the best of us? We follow in the example of the two most famous people to ever don a coat of many colors: Joseph, whose story is told in the book of Genesis, and Dolly Parton.

Joseph was the firstborn son of Jacob and Rachel. Given the royal treatment from an early age, Joseph was favored by his dad. He was favored so much, in fact, that Jacob gave him an expensive "coat of many colors" (Genesis 37:3 KJV), one that reminded his half brothers just how favored he was. But what started as simple jealousy turned into full-on murderous rage when Joseph told them of a dream he had, a dream that foreshadowed his vocational calling, a dream he'd interpreted to mean his brothers would one day bow to him. So the half brothers dragged Joseph into the desert intent on killing him before ultimately stripping him of his coat and selling him to some passing tradesmen headed to Egypt.

Joseph again found himself in a wealthy house, but this time, the wealthy man was not his father, and he was not the favored son. He was a slave, a piece of property owned by an Egyptian nobleman, Potiphar (Genesis 39). And though he could have frozen in fear, Joseph didn't. He worked his way up the ladder in Potiphar's house. It wasn't an optimal life. (Understatement of the century.) It wasn't the vocational path he'd chosen. Still, he gave everything to it. And when Potiphar's wife noticed Joseph was well built and handsome, she begged him to bed her. (Even Joseph had his #metoo moment.) Day after day he refused her advances and harassment, until she tried to force Joseph into her bed. He fled, but he left his coat in her hands. It was this coat that would serve as *Exhibit A* in the charge of attempted rape levied by Potiphar's wife.

Joseph couldn't catch a break. He found himself in prison, alone, in a strange land. He must have been full of fear, but what did he do?

He made himself of service in the prison, and as a result, he received promotion after promotion after promotion by the warden of the jail until Joseph found himself in charge of it all. (Talk about a shift in the winds.) Finally, at the end of two very long years in prison and after earning a reputation for being a bit of a dream interpreter, he was called on by Pharaoh to interpret two royal dreams (Genesis 41). Standing before the most powerful man in the world, a man who could end Joseph's life if he was displeased with the interpretation, Joseph called on God for help, and God gave him the meaning. Seven years of famine were coming, Joseph said, and Egypt needed to prepare. Recognizing Joseph's wisdom, Pharaoh promoted Joseph and put him in charge of preparing for the coming famine.

Time after time, Joseph was met with external resistance, resistance that could have allowed fear to take hold. But time after time, Joseph pushed back the fear—the fear of slavery, of false accusation, of imprisonment, of standing before the ruler of the known world and he dedicated himself to the task in front of him. Time after time, God blessed him, eventually making him the manager for the resources of all of Egypt (perhaps the equivalent to the chairman of the Federal Reserve today). And that's when everything came full circle. The famine hadn't just struck Egypt. It had spread to the surrounding region, including the place where Joseph's family lived. And when his brothers—the same ones who'd sold him into slavery—came looking for food, Joseph provided enough for them. In fact, he invited his whole family to make their home in Egypt, the land of plenty (Genesis 45).

Not once do we read of fear limiting Joseph's vocational calling, nor did it disrupt his faith calling. Had things been unfair? Sure. Did person after person sell him, attack him, harass him, levy false accusations against him, and imprison him? Absolutely. Did he have any idea what he was doing as he moved from job to job to job? Probably not. But knowing God had equipped him and would continue to equip him, standing firm in his faith calling and trusting in God, Joseph pressed on. It was that pressing on that allowed him to care for the people through his unique vocational calling.

Most of us don't have trials of biblical proportions as Joseph did. (If you do, let me start a GoFundMe page for you, please!) Our tribulations are the more run-of-the-mill, day-to-day sorts of struggles. Still, they are our own, and when we're in the middle of them, we can find ourselves paralyzed, even blinded by fear. But if we're rooted in our faith calling—reminding ourselves we're first called to love God and love people—and if we keep pressing through the fear and into the vocational calling God has laid out for us, we can muscle through any circumstance. We *can* press through the fear. If we don't, we won't find the gold God has for us.

What Dolly Parton Taught Me about Fear (and Knocking on Bathroom Doors)

Over the course of my career, I've met more than a few people who've muscled through fear to pursue their vocational calling, but only one shared Joseph's fashion sense, "Coat of Many Colors" singer and country music icon Dolly Parton. But Dolly and I didn't meet in the traditional way journalists meet celebrities. We didn't meet for an exclusive interview or backstage at an ABC event. We met in a much more awkward fashion—when I barged through the door of her bathroom stall.

I was in my own world, happy and humming a tune in the moments before anchoring *Good Morning America* on a weekday morning alongside George Stephanopoulos and Michael Strahan. I walked into the bathroom, made my way to the bank of stalls. The middle one occupied, I pushed on the slightly ajar door of the last stall. I must have pushed a little too hard, because the stall door swung open and hit someone in the shoulder. That someone was the Queen of Country, Dolly Parton. I looked down, and before I could keep the words from slipping off my lips, I said, "It's Dolly Parton!"

I turned to the other stall, now verbalizing my internal monologue.

"I just walked in on Dolly Parton! I'm so embarrassed!"

Everything froze except Dolly. She emerged from the stall with a million-dollar smile. I apologized profusely, to which she replied, "Don't worry about it, sweetie." I stood there frozen as she made her way to the sink, washed her hands, and scooted out the door for her performance later that morning on *GMA*.

My cheeks turned to fire, my stomach into a knot. I'd walked in on Dolly doing her business. Why hadn't I looked under the stall? Why hadn't I knocked? Why had I pushed so hard on that door? *What was wrong with me?* I finished up in the restroom, then walked back to the studio, head down, shaking the nerves out of my fingers.

Dolly had come on the show that morning to promote her literacy program, a passion of hers after growing up in a home where her father couldn't read or write. I watched Michael interview her, and she spoke about the book she'd written, *Coat of Many Colors*, a book based on her own life story. Dolly was raised in a poor mountain family from Tennessee, and her parents couldn't afford new coats for all the kids. So her mother bought a box of old rags, which she turned into fabric squares and stitched together to make a coat of many colors for young Dolly. She shared how her classmates made fun of her patchwork coat, of her poverty. And though the criticism might have been enough to undercut her self-confidence, though it could have made her shrink back in fear, according to the book (and the song by the same name), Parton held her head high and pushed through in confidence, knowing she'd been given everything she needed in love.

As I listened, I held back tears. What a message: Love fueled her confidence, allowing her to push past the fear.

After the interview, I passed Dolly in the hall, and I did my best to keep my head down. She stopped me, though, looked into my eyes, and laughed. Again, I said how sorry I was. Dolly didn't miss a beat. Reaching out and taking my arm, she said, "Girls that pee together, stay together." That sense of humor, that charm—what a rare thing these days.

When I consider Dolly's life, I see a woman who has endured more than I. She didn't let poverty and the bullying of others rob her of her self-confidence, and times being what they were when she was coming up, I'm sure she suffered her share of harassment and unfair treatment (this is just the reality for most working women). But she overcame the odds and made it as a country artist. Why? As she put it in an interview with George Stephanopoulos years earlier, she'd succeeded because "My desire was always greater than my fear."

There it is, the antidote: Cultivate a desire bigger than fear.

We'll all experience the external pressures that trigger fear, especially as we push into our vocational calling. You might not have the money to pursue education. Others might tell you that you're not good enough or smart enough or bold enough. You might be told you're too small a fish in too big a market. You might be harassed, sabotaged, set up. The people you try to serve might not appreciate you, might tell you you're doing everything wrong (a particularly poignant reality for those of us who are mothers). But when these external realities come against you, don't freeze in fear. Instead, cultivate a desire greater than your fear. Cultivate a faith bigger than fear too, and remember that if God calls you, he'll equip you. Just as he called and equipped Joseph, and Dolly Parton, and me, he'll do that for you too. And as you believe this reality, as you speak it over your life, you'll begin to see the truth. Your vocational calling is much bigger than the fear that limits you.

The Danger of White-Hot Desire

If my life up to that point was any indication, I should have called it quits in those early days in Dayton. Seasoned broadcasters were working on TV in Dayton—I had no business trying to cut my teeth in such a large market.

Shouldn't that have made me feel insufficient before I even started? And the female news anchor who had berated my journalistic skills in front of the entire news team— shouldn't that tongue-lashing by a seasoned veteran have made me feel unworthy, invaluable? Shouldn't that fear of not fitting in have led me to quit? What about the co-worker who meant to intimidate me, who harassed me and sabotaged my tapes—wasn't he trying to force me out? Why didn't his bullying beat me into quitting?

> **When external realities come against you, don't freeze in fear. Instead, cultivate a desire greater than your fear.**

The odds were stacked against me in Dayton, and yet I had a desire that outmatched anyone's attempt to hold me back. I had a desire that was bigger than my fear. That desire made all the difference.

If only I had learned to keep that desire firmly rooted in my faith calling, maybe that white-hot desire wouldn't have almost burned me out and burned up my marriage.

But sometimes, we learn the most important lessons through the messes we make.

CHAPTER 6

Out of the Comfort Zone, through the Fear

Pulling together a list of must-interview guests for a faith podcast isn't a cakewalk. We live in an era of private faith, a day and age in which any expression of belief in God—whether Christian, Jewish, Muslim, or otherwise—is often taboo. In fact, in media circles, many don't want to hear about your faith, much less report about it. You can talk about the game-winning catch, your latest project, the headlines . . . But if you mention God, Jesus, Allah, or Buddha? Yeah . . . that's probably not going to make the air.

Stepping away to create a faith podcast in this industry seemed a tricky proposition, but there were plenty of spiritual people in the world around me. How many would be willing to go on a podcast and discuss their faith, their religion? Who could say? But sitting at my desk a few weeks after my conversation with James, I scribbled out a list of names. At the top of that list was Robin Roberts, my longtime co-worker at ABC.

From the beginning, Robin was a bright light. She was quick with a smile or an encouraging word. And she never shied away from expressing her faith. Whether on *Good Morning America* or in public speeches, she'd never been afraid to tell a good God story. She was fond of saying, "My parents raised me to believe in the three *Ds*—discipline, determination, and Da Lord."

Robin had been serious about her faith even as she climbed the ranks in broadcasting, and when she began working for *Good Morning America* in 2002—the largest stage in broadcasting—she continued to be who she was. An unashamed, unabashed, outspoken God-lover. In her early days at *GMA*, the producers had created a segment about the cast members' morning routines. When asked if she had a morning ritual, Roberts shared her daily prayer, the last thing she whispers before walking out the door each day: "The light of God surrounds me, the love of God enfolds me, the power of God protects me, the presence of God watches over me; wherever I am, God is." To ABC's credit, they didn't shy away from Roberts's prayer, running it on *GMA*, and after they did, calls poured in requesting a copy of that prayer.

Roberts had also battled and beaten cancer twice—breast cancer in 2002 and myelodysplastic syndrome, a form of pre-leukemia, in 2012. Through it all, she'd been outspoken about her faith, which had carried her through, and it had been an inspiration to so many, including me. If it had just been those things, it would have been enough for her to top my list of prospective interview candidates. But this wasn't just about Robin's public persona. This was personal.

Within days of my meeting with James in the spring of 2018, I made my way to Robin's *GMA* office, just after the show had finished taping.

I knocked on her door, and she welcomed me with her usual smile (wearing her post-show green frog slippers, of course). I asked if she had a few minutes, and generous as she is with her time, she invited me in and asked me to sit. Over the next hour (so much for a minute), I told her I was officially quitting *The View*, and that I'd be stepping down from my duties as the weekend co-anchor of *GMA*. Her smile evened out, her brow flattened. What would I do at the network? she asked. I wasn't exactly sure, I said, but I wanted to do something new, something that gave me a Monday-through-Friday schedule so I could spend more time with my husband and kids. I wanted to do something with faith too. Maybe a podcast. She wondered how I felt about the prospect of leaving my anchoring responsibilities and starting something new. I didn't hold back.

"I'm scared out of my mind. What if it doesn't work out? What if I fail?"

She smiled and shook her head. "Don't allow fear to prevent you from walking into your destiny," she said. There was such confidence, such purpose in her voice. As we wrapped up our conversation, she asked if she could pray for me, and as she did, something happened. My fear began to loosen.

If Robin Roberts believed in me, I could do anything.

Robin walks into the studio on an ordinary Monday, smiling. Beaming, really. She's relaxed (isn't she always?) and she's wearing a purple hoodie with *#BLESSED* emblazoned across the chest. We exchange hellos and a hug, and she sits across the desk from me, ready to roll.

We begin recording, and I introduce Robin to the listeners, though she doesn't need much introduction. I share the common threads of our careers, how we both came from sports backgrounds and made our way through smaller markets. I tell listeners how Robin made it to the pinnacle of sports broadcasting—ESPN—before moving to ABC. I also share how she'd been so encouraging when I'd told her I was making the move from the anchor desk to this podcast, and she remembers what she told me: *Don't allow fear to get in the way of your destiny.*

I begin peppering her with questions about the role of faith in her childhood, and Robin shares how God and church formed the foundation of her family. The child of a Tuskegee Airman, Robin and her family moved from base to base, but everywhere they went, there was one constant—faith in God. And when the family moved to Keesler Air Force base in Biloxi, Mississippi, her mother and father not only attended the church service on the base, they started one—a "Soul Service" for African Americans stationed in Biloxi. The Soul Service provided a safe place for black men and women to sing, pray, study the Bible, and express their faith at a particularly turbulent time in American history. Roberts was affected by all that exposure to faith, she says, and it became her own, a faith she's never left.

"What do you believe?" I ask.

She doesn't hold back. "I believe in God the almighty, maker of heaven and earth, and in Jesus Christ his only son, our Lord."

Church wasn't just a childhood thing, she shares. As her career moved her from town to town—Hattiesburg, Biloxi, Nashville, Atlanta, Bristol, New York—she's made church a priority (though it's been hard to attend church after the passing of her mother, she admits). She shares how her faith has pulled her through both of her battles with cancer, how it has made her a better sister, a better partner, a better person. Her faith has influenced everything, something I've always known about Robin.

Would people know that about me?

Robin approaches the topic of vocation, and my ears perk up. She shares her two favorite sports figures, tennis players Billie Jean King and Arthur Ashe. Both lived lives bigger than their vocation, she said. They used their platforms to do good. And both encouraged her to step onto bigger stages, bigger platforms so she could make an impact on the world. She remembers a conversation with Ashe, how he'd told her, "If at the end of the day, people only say about you, 'Boy, she was a heck of a broadcaster,' you haven't fulfilled your mission."

There it is, the common thread. Just like David Shedd had said, our vocational callings are meant for something bigger. They're meant to advance our purpose, our faith calling—to be our unique vehicle by which we love God and others. They're meant to be rooted in and flow from our faith calling. And when that happens, it's God's love and our mandate to love others that motivates us to push through our fear and move into new opportunities, new areas of influence. It doesn't become so much about *what we do*, but rather *who we're doing it for.*

> **Our vocational callings are meant to advance our purpose, our faith calling—to be our unique vehicle by which we love God and others.**

After rising through the ranks of ESPN, Robin was invited to host the news for the morning segment of *Good Morning America*. But when ABC asked her to join the host team at *Good Morning America*, Robin admits she almost turned it down. She was in sports, had always been in sports, and wanted to stay in sports. Besides, what did she know about hosting a national morning show? And if it didn't work out, if she traded in her position at the sports desk for a dead end, then what? She gives it to me straight:

> I was loving my comfort zone. I wasn't just in it. I was *all up in it* and loving it. . . . I don't want to say I reached a glass ceiling at ESPN, but then I realized there was just so much I was going to be able to do. . . . But I was interviewing Billie Jean King, and I remember telling her, "Billie they're offering me this full-time position at *Good Morning America*," and I think part of me wanted her to say, "You can't leave sports!" But she was just the opposite. "Snap out of it! What are you thinking?! It's a bigger stage! You're still going to be

able to cover sports." And then I realized I was limiting myself by being in just the sports world.

There it was again, more alignment with my interview with David Shedd. Robin was a gifted anchor, and she had an innate curiosity, but she also had someone like Billie Jean King speaking life into this new branch of her vocational calling. I share the insight with Robin, then say, "Sometimes other people have the dream for you before you have it for yourself because you've allowed your fear to paralyze you."

"Amen," Roberts says. "And fear just needs the eye of a needle to get through and it just consumes your very being. So many fears keep us sidelined."

We wrap up the interview, say our good-byes, and as I walk to my office to grab my wallet, I consider Robin's story, how she'd been in her comfort zone. "All up in it and loving it," in fact. Afraid of stepping out, it had taken the encouragement of a trusted friend and mentor, someone seeing the dream for her, before she'd take the step out of her comfort zone, through fear, and into a new opportunity.

That's what I was praying for my own journey of faith, that by stepping out of my comfort zone, by exploring a new branch of my vocational calling, I'd find new opportunity, maybe an opportunity where I could experience the love of God more and share it with others.

Finding My Comfort Zone—from Dayton to Chicago

How had I gotten to New York City, to this interview with Robin? I'd stepped out of my comfort zone, one move at a time.

After taking my first job in Dayton, I busted my tail trying to prove I belonged, and started putting feelers out in bigger markets. I wound up landing a job at the ABC affiliate in Cincinnati, WCPO-TV. It was there I would find myself doubting everything. My calling. My marriage. Who I was.

Before the move from Dayton to Cincinnati, I'd already been covering sports in southwest Ohio, including Cincinnati. On occasion, I covered the Reds (Cincinnati's Major League Baseball team) and the Bengals (the city's NFL franchise), and while reporting at those games, I rubbed shoulders with folks from the area network affiliates. As I did, I began to develop a feel for the market. It was larger—the thirty-fifth-largest market in the country—and their crews were a little more seasoned, a little more polished. (Most of their reporters didn't have to shoot their own material.) Though I enjoyed living in Dayton and was grateful to Ian, who'd given me my first shot, I took a hard look at the reporters in Cincy, and a thought took hold. I could make it there.

Through the grapevine, I'd heard there was an opening at the news desk of a Cincinnati affiliate, so I polished up my résumé and made a tape, and submitted it all to that Cincinnati station, not knowing whether I even had what it took to land the spot. But weeks later, I received the sort of phone call that might have pushed all my fear-of-failure buttons, one that might have short-circuited my career years earlier.

"We're sorry," the news director said from the other side of the phone. "We just don't think you're ready."

Not ready?

Add more fuel to my already white-hot ambition.

A few weeks passed, and I heard of another opening, one that better suited my skill set. The weekend sports anchor from the ABC affiliate at WCPO-TV, Kathrine Nero, was jumping from the sports desk to the news desk, and they were looking for a woman to fill her spot—even though no one could ever take Kathrine's place. She was a beloved mainstay in the community. Still, there was a hole in their lineup, and I knew I was the one to fill it.

Only forty-eight hours after hearing of the opening, and after only a year in Dayton, I made a gutsy move. I drove the fifty minutes south on I-75 to meet the news director, Bob Morford. It was a brief meeting, one in which he offered me the job on the spot. I accepted. And with that, I was a sports anchor and reporter in a top-35 market.

John and I had already talked it out. It was the break we'd been waiting for. And though it'd mean more drive time, though it put additional strain on our young and already fragile marriage, it seemed to check all the boxes.

John could keep his job coaching basketball. Check.

I would move up the broadcasting food chain. Check.

More money. Check.

Cincinnati could have been a lot of things. It could have been the place where I rooted into my faith, where I did my best to understand my faith calling. It could have been the place where I began using my growing platform for a purpose. It could have been the place our young marriage flourished, the place where we learned to love each other sacrificially. It could have been, but sadly, it wasn't.

Details matter, even when they're not meant to be shared in a public forum. So I'll share this: As I chased more career opportunities, I set out to burn our marriage down. I moved out and wanted to move on, and had John not been steadfast, had he not fought for our marriage, I might have succeeded.

> **As I chased more career opportunities, I set out to burn our marriage down. I moved out and wanted to move on, and had John not fought for our marriage, I might have succeeded.**

In 2005, in what could have been the smoldering ruins of a marriage, John and I decided we'd scrape the remains of our marriage together and try again. To do it, though, we'd need a change of scenery, a change of city, but I'd only been in Cincinnati a few years, and I was all of twenty-nine. Did I have enough experience to move to an even bigger market, maybe a top ten? How would I even go about it? I wasn't sure exactly, but I'd learned enough to know that a good television agent could help. So I did a little research, a little asking around, and I came up with the names of two very qualified media agents. One was a big-time New York talent agent who represents the likes of Don Lemon, Robin Roberts, and David Muir. The other, Matthew Kingsley, had been with a big agency, but he'd gone out on his own. At the time, his client roster didn't boast the heavy hitters, but he was a man of faith. And I was drawn to that.

I interviewed both of them. The New York agent carried himself with an air of importance, a selling point in this business—but there was something about Matthew. We'd talked candidly about our common faith, something I desperately needed more of in my life. Still unsure who might be best at getting me out of Cincinnati, though, I flipped a coin.

Heads, I'd go with the bright-lights, big-city agent.

Tails, Matthew.

I flipped the coin, which came up heads. Without hesitation, I said, "Best two out of three." That's when I knew It had to be Matthew.

Hiring Matthew might have been a career-saving move, though I didn't know it then. In no time, he delivered an opportunity with WMAQ-TV, the NBC affiliate in Chicago. It was the third largest media market in America, and I'd be the weekend sports anchor, he said. (And for the record, I wouldn't have to show my chest to do it.) There was a down side, though. John would have to quit his job—which he was willing to do, he said. He was willing to do anything to get us out of Cincinnati so we could rebuild our marriage. Besides, he said, Chicago was only three hours from my folks in Michigan and two from his parents in Indiana. If we had kids, wouldn't we want to live closer to our parents?

I took another small step out of my comfort zone and took the job. I anchored the sports desk Saturday and Sunday, and throughout the week, I interviewed Chicago sports personalities, filed reports, and attended production meetings. Long gone were the days of running the prompter, hauling my own equipment, one-man-banding, and trying to balance the sports desk. In fact, I wasn't even allowed to touch the equipment in Chicago because it was a union shop, and only certain employees could use particular equipment. There were bigger shows with bigger budgets and bigger crews and bigger responsibilities. Could I hack it? Was I good enough? I wasn't sure, but when the question came calling, when it filled me with fear, I did what I'd always done. I put in extra effort, worked like a madwoman to show I belonged through success and achievement. And as I achieved more and more, as the success built, I found the fear of failure retreating, just like it always had.

Still trying to regain our footing, John and I settled into a new city. We went to Cubs games at Wrigley, explored the lakefront, and discovered Chicago-style pizza. (Which I maintain is hands-down better than any New York-style pizza in Manhattan, though you need a few days to recover after eating it.) And as we learned to love each other in ways we could understand, as we learned to forgive the seemingly unforgivable, magic happened. I discovered I was pregnant with our first child, our daughter Caroline.

Talk about stepping out of my comfort zone.

How I'd balance motherhood and a demanding career I wasn't sure, but I didn't let the fear slow me down. I pushed harder, did more. (In fact, early in my pregnancy, while battling severe nausea, I covered the Chicago Bears in Super Bowl XLI in 2007.) But when Caroline came, when I looked into her eyes for the first time, something shifted. My singular focus—my vocational calling—broadened, even if I couldn't say exactly why or how. In that hospital room I held my firstborn child, and I stared into her eyes while John stood over me, stroking my hair. Family. Career. Could I do it all? How?

Marriage, mothering, a demanding career—over the year that followed, I never could seem to make them balance. I moved from sporting event to sporting event, weekend to weekend, interview to interview, shipping my breast milk cross-country on dry ice when I was on long assignments. And through it all, I wondered whether I was giving enough to Caroline, enough to John, enough to my job. And in this season of very normal, very typical questions about work–life balance, I received the best news. Unexpected news. I was pregnant again.

It was an unexpected pregnancy because we'd had a miscarriage before Caroline, and it had taken us seven years to bring her into the world. But as I prepared to welcome my second-born, JJ, I heard new inner voices.

I can't balance work and family.

I can't have it all.

After everything I've done to John, I don't deserve this.

I listened to those voices, to the self-criticism, and I took them to heart. And for the first time since college, I wanted nothing more than to quit everything. But since I couldn't quit, the next best thing was jumping ship.

I'd been a hot commodity in Chicago just a year before JJ was born, and I could have made a lateral move to any sports desk in the city. But I didn't want to make a lateral move. I wanted to move to the news desk or a morning show, to something that would give me more flexibility to be with John and the family. And to add even more specificity, I wanted to do it in Chicago. So when a CBS network executive from New York called, then flew me out to interview for a position on their network morning show, I hadn't been sure I wanted it. So what did I do? I self-sabotaged the interview. It was so bad, in fact, that during the interview the then-president of the network, Sean McManus, asked if I even wanted this job. My response was straightforward: "Only if it allows me to stay in Chicago."

I probably don't need to tell you how that worked out.

In this new season in Chicago, this season in which I'd be balancing work with mothering two children, I was pretty clear with God: "Hey, God, if I'm gonna keep doing this reporting gig, it has to be in Chicago, my comfort zone. Okay? Thanks." (Not one of my finer, obedient moments.)

For a year, my agent, Matthew, tried to find me something more flexible in Chicago. For a year the doors closed. Every single one. When I auditioned for the morning talk show *Windy City Live*, I was told I wasn't right for a talk show. (Ironic, since I went on to co-host *The View*.) Even the doors at my own station were closed. When I asked my news director and general manager in Chicago to move to the morning show, my news director told me, "You'll never be seen as anything more than a sports anchor." Every trail was a dead end. If I wanted to stay in Chicago, the city I'd grown so comfortable in, I'd have to stay at the sports desk, and that wasn't best for my young family. It looked like there was only one option. I'd have to step outside my comfort zone.

How to Be a "Democratic Shill" and Other Ways of Stepping Outside Your Comfort Zone

If it's worth having, it's worth fighting for—it's one of those sayings we've heard ad nauseam. But it's true. Look at your own life. Anything worth having has come from sacrifice, hasn't it? And sacrifice requires us to step out of our comfort zones and into the hard stuff of life. It requires us to stare down our fears.

If journalism teaches you anything, it's the art of breaking out of your comfort zone. Pursuing bigger markets, bigger stories, and bigger opportunities requires risk. You put yourself out there again and again, each time facing the fear that you might fail, and many times, you do. But receiving bigger assignments requires developing a high risk-tolerance. It requires stepping out of your comfort zone. And though it's an easy thing to say from this side of the anchor desk, it's not so easy to live out.

I could have stayed in Dayton forever, could have been content to be on the air in a mid-sized market making minimum wage. And even though Cincinnati was an unknown market with unknown challenges, I pushed out of my comfort zone, walked through whatever fears I might have had, and made the move. And when it came time to move from Cincinnati to Chicago, the same was true.

Stepping out of our comfort zone and into our vocational calling isn't just about new job opportunities and better positions, though. Sometimes, our vocational callings require us to endure hardship or harsh criticism. And as a reporter—especially one with a Christian worldview—I receive my fair share of public criticism, none of which is ever comfortable.

> **Stepping out of our comfort zone and into our vocational calling isn't just about new job opportunities. Sometimes, our vocational callings require us to endure hardship or criticism.**

For instance, consider an interview I did with Beto O'Rourke, a Democratic senatorial candidate for Texas during the 2018 election. Conservative Christians accused me of going soft on a Democratic candidate. Detractors called me "Libtard," and a "Democratic shill." And those were just the G-rated names. On the other side, Democrats accused me of bias and being disingenuous. Talk about pushing into a career with no comfort zone.

If the public quips on social media are bad, the character attacks in mass media are even worse. Tabloids like *Page Six* have run slanderous stories about me. (More on that in chapter 8.) There have been times when my career was a hot mess fueled by the negativity and criticism of others, and in those seasons, a comfort zone was a distant memory.

If you live in the real world, there will be moments when you have to step out of your comfort zone, or when you'll be pushed out of your comfort zone, as you pursue your vocational calling. Though your fear (or other people) might tell you you're not good enough, or qualified enough, or capable enough for that next job, you might need to apply anyway. Though the next step in your vocational calling may subject you to criticism or discomfort, you might have to wade into that discomfort in order to receive the rewards of pushing through the hardship. (This might be especially true if your vocational calling is as a stay-at-home mother. Those kids—they can be more brutal than any dumpster fire at work, can't they?) Stepping out of your comfort zone might require you to muster up the courage to take a risk, make a move, face criticism and brush it off, forgive the detractors even when they don't ask for forgiveness, and surge ahead. It might require you to step into things that are truly fearsome.

> In the darkest days of our marriage, when John and I felt there was nothing worth fighting for, we stepped out of our comfort zones. And it led to the most amazing rewards.

What's true in our vocational calling is true in our day-to-day lives too. In the darkest days of our marriage, when John and I felt there was nothing worth fighting for, we stepped out of our comfort zones. Was there fear that we didn't have what it took to make it work? Sure. Would it have been easier, maybe even more comfortable, to go our own ways? Maybe. Still, we stepped out of our comfort zones and into that fear, and though it was the hardest thing we had ever done, it led to the most amazing rewards. It led to a rich love, a deep companionship, and three wonderful children.

Journeys of Faith Begin Outside Our Comfort Zones

Jumping out of our comfort zones and into something new, something we can't quite see yet—could there be a better definition of faith? (Remember the words of Dr. King from chapter 1? "Faith is taking the first step, even when you don't see the whole staircase.")

Throughout the Bible, women and men left their comfort zones, pushed through the fear, and discovered amazing possibilities. We read of Noah in Genesis 6–9, who followed God's call to build an enormous boat. His neighbors probably mocked him for it, might even have called him crazy. But what was the result of Noah's obedience? He and his entire family were saved from the flood God brought to destroy the world.

Esther—the Jewish beauty queen with a book named for her in the Old Testament—was called to enter the harem of the Persian king. (Ugh. Talk about a job description that objectifies women.) She left the comforts of her daily life, sacrificed her dignity and Jewish pride, and walked headlong into the daunting prospect of being in a strange man's palace. Eventually rising to become the queen, Esther received word from her uncle of a genocidal plot by one of the king's officials to kill all the Jews, Esther's people. So Esther, who was loved by the king, used her position and influence to disrupt the plan, save the people, and bring the genocidal schmuck to justice.

Then there's Mary, the mother of Jesus. Just a teenager—and unmarried at that—she obediently abandoned the comfort of her average life and agreed to carry the Son of God. Like Noah, she sacrificed her reputation, her pride, her everyday life. She sacrificed all of it for something greater, and as a result, she was the one to bring Jesus into the world.

Our sacrifices won't top those of the biblical characters. You probably won't have to trade your reputation for a hammer and nails, probably won't have to build a giant escape ark. (But if you do, give me a call; I'd like the exclusive interview.) I doubt you'll sacrifice your sense of nationalistic pride to become a secret agent in the house of a foreign king so that you can uncover a genocidal plot. (Again, if that's where God moves you, call me.) You won't have to carry the Son of God.

Still, big things will require us to step out of our comfort zones, step through our fears, and step into something we couldn't previously have imagined. Outside our comfort zones—that's where we'll find God waiting.

Are you at a vocational crossroads? Maybe you're considering taking a promotion, switching roles in your current company, or changing industries altogether. Perhaps you're considering leaving the workforce to become a stay-at-home parent. Are you afraid of moving out of your comfort zone to pursue that next step? Does the prospect of failure, or of doing something new, scare you? Join the club. It's not only normal, it's expected.

But spend some time considering your vocational calling and what sacrifices you'll have to make in order to pursue it. Then, cultivate a desire that is bigger than the fear of stepping out, remembering that when God calls you vocationally, he'll equip you. But he's not just equipping you for a job, he's equipping you to share his love through your job, through a unique position only you can fill.

Robin encouraged me—*Don't let your fear prevent you from walking into your destiny*. She encouraged me to move out of my comfort zone and into the unknown. But she wasn't the only one who encouraged me along the way. In fact, had it not been for my agent's wife, I never would have stayed in broadcasting, never would have taken the leap to New York City.

It was that leap that would ultimately bring me to the end of self, and make me confront my biggest fears. It was that leap that would lead me to understand the ultimate truth—that my true identity wasn't found in what I did, but rather in who I was.

But that was a lesson that would take me years to learn.

CHAPTER 7

An Impostor in New York

Walking from the studio after the interview with Robin, I'm famished and looking for a healthy snack, something like a beef stick and bag of salt-and-vinegar potato chips. (That's my version of healthy.) I walk toward a little bodega in Times Square, just down the street from where *Good Morning America* broadcasts live Monday through Friday. As I do, I consider Robin, how she was *all up in her comfort zone* before she made the step to *GMA*. I guess I had been the same in Chicago, though motherhood seemed to be drawing me out of my comfort zone more and more. And as the doors to achieving work–life balance closed in Chicago, doubts set in, and with them the fear.

What if I'm really not good enough to anchor the news desk?

What if I've screwed up my marriage and my family beyond repair and I can't figure out how to fix it?

Am I even worthy of this work, this family?

Robin's comment—*Fear just needs the eye of a needle to get through and it just consumes your very being*—how true that had been in my own life. And it had almost disrupted my vocational calling.

I make my way into the bodega, head for the potato chip aisle, and remember how I'd pushed through the fear to get to New York in the first place. Or more accurately, I'd been pushed through the fear by Jan Jeffcoat, my agent's wife. When I was on the edge of giving up in Chicago, Jan called, said she'd heard I'd considered quitting. She wasn't having it. As tenacious as she is convincing, she laid into me.

"You can't quit," she said. "Remember Jesus' words from the book of Matthew? 'You are the light of the world. A city on a hill can't be hidden.'" Then she added her own spin on the Scriptures: "You don't light a candle and put it under a bowl. Paula, you can't hide your God-given talent."

It was a simple word of encouragement, one I'll never forget, and it restored some shred of self-confidence, enough to help me push back the voices of fear and take a step out of my comfortable Midwestern life and into something new. So months later, when New York came calling a second time, I was ready.

Ready to step out of my comfort zone and past the fear?

Yes.

Ready to step into a new job, even if I didn't know whether I could hack it?

Maybe.

Ready to move ahead, even if the path to what I so wanted—a comfortable work-life balance in Chicago—wasn't readily apparent? I wasn't thrilled about the possibility of that, but if God opened the doors, I knew I had to listen.

I step to the counter to pay for my snacks and I smile, thinking about the way Jan's little encouragement pushed me forward, how it had been just what I needed in the moment. And as I turn back toward the studio, I think about all the sacrifices I've made to get here—time, presence, and even my own identity. Though there were things I'd do differently if given the opportunity, I was glad I stepped through the fear that had threatened to paralyze me.

Jan Jeffcoat had been right, of course. Looking back, I could see God leading me into journalism through the prodding of my teachers and professors. God had confirmed my vocational calling by opening doors in Dayton, and opening Ian's heart to putting me on the air. God had allowed me opportunity after opportunity and had encouraged me all along the way. And when I was on the edge of giving up, he sent a *very loud* reminder through Jan.

God bless Jan Jeffcoat.

In the days following our conversation in Chicago, I couldn't shake the conviction that I was supposed to continue in broadcasting. And though I was tired, maybe a little burned out, I'd decided not to run anymore. In that new resolve, while lying in bed a week after my conversation with Jan, I heard a small internal voice, something nearly audible: *"Get ready. I have something big for you."* I didn't have to ask who it was or what it meant. I knew it was God. But out of options as I was, I knew I needed to pay attention to any opportunities that popped up, especially audacious ones. And it wouldn't take long.

A day or two passed. Maybe a week. And as if on cue, Matthew called. He'd been contacted by Barbara Fedida, an executive at ABC News, who wanted to interview me for a position.

"Fedida? The same one who interviewed me a year ago for the CBS position that I sabotaged?"

"Same one," he said. "She's moved to ABC and she'd really like you to join the team."

Barbara was persistent, I'd give her that much. And could the timing be any stranger? I'd only just had the conversation with Jan, only just heard from God. I figured I'd be a fool to pass over all these signs, so I agreed to take the interview. What could it hurt?

A week later, I was sitting across the table from Barbara Fedida at ABC's headquarters in Manhattan. She was looking for a new anchor for the overnight news broadcast, *World News Now*, she said. It'd been a job with a lot of turnover over the last couple years, a revolving door of interim anchors. It was a hard shift, she recognized, but it was a great place to start working my way up in the national spotlight. So many had gotten their start there—Anderson Cooper, Juju Chang, David Muir. I should see the job as a steppingstone.

"Are you interested in moving to New York yet?"

"I'm not opposed to it," I said, and when the words escaped my mouth, I knew. It was time to leave my comfort zone, to step away from the sports desk in Chicago and into the unknown. It was time to become a very small fish in the very large, competitive, and sometimes aggressive sea of national broadcasting.

It was time to become a very small fish in the very large, competitive, and sometimes aggressive sea of national broadcasting.

Returning to Chicago, John and I sat on the couch discussing the move. There was a lengthy list of cons. We'd have to put our home on the market, and we'd likely take a loss. John, who was now working in real estate, would have to put his career on pause for me. Again. We'd have to leave the comfort of our city, our church, the friends we'd made over the past six years. We'd have to move more than a day's drive away from our family; our kids were just four and two. I'd have to work overnight, limiting my time with John and the kids. And although there was a slight bump in my salary—not enough to compensate for the cost of living differential—was it enough to justify making the jump? Probably not, especially considering we'd be a single-income family until John found another gig. And then there was New York City itself, the city I liked to visit but *loved* to leave. Could our young family thrive in that kind of hustle?

Cons discussed, we turned to the list of pros. It was a very short list: the job at ABC was a bigger opportunity. It was an exciting pro, one full of possibility. John and I both sensed God calling us to New York. So, knowing God would be with us, recognizing a desire that was bigger than any of my personal fears, and ready to jump out of my comfort zone, I called Matthew Kingsley, my agent, and told him the news. I wanted the job.

"I'll take care of it," he said. "Pack your bags."

Within weeks, John and I put our house on the market, loaded up a moving truck, sold or donated whatever wouldn't fit in it, and set off for New York. Were we insane? Maybe. But we trusted there was something bigger waiting for us.

I hit the ground running, leaving John at home to unpack boxes and tend to the children in a tiny two-bedroom, one-bath apartment on the Upper West Side of Manhattan. It wasn't the long-term solution, and John desperately wanted to find a job and be productive in the city, but true to his word that he'd move anywhere, do anything to support my career, he accepted the short-term role of stay-at-home dad. (I hope you're beginning to see the thread here. John is a bona fide saint.)

Not long after I arrived, I made my way to an anchor luncheon. Clenching my fists in hopes of settling my nerves, I entered the meeting room, which had wide, sweeping views of Manhattan. I looked around the room and freaked out a bit. Diane Sawyer and Barbara Walters were there, both living legends in broadcast journalism. Katie Couric was chatting it up with someone I didn't know. Robin Roberts, one of my sports broadcasting heroes, was there. So was George Stepha-nopoulos. David Muir. Charlie Gibson. I looked around the room, shook my hands out a couple of times before wading in. Was this real? How unqualified was I to be with all these iconic personalities? Was it too late to go back to Chicago?

Had I known how lovely, approachable, and mostly humble this cast of characters was, I might not have been so nervous. Still, though the fear was rising, I didn't run. Instead, I set my jaw, put on a smile, and waded in, determined to show everyone I belonged. Sure, God had brought me here, but he would help those who helped themselves. Right?

I don't remember all the details of the luncheon, which isn't necessarily a bad thing. Broccoli in the teeth? That's a memorable detail. Making a ridiculous comment about world events in front of so many brilliant newscasters? That's a memorable detail. Walking through your first luncheon with toilet paper stuck to your heel? A memorable detail. The fact that I don't have any such memories? I consider that a win. But as I left that truly lovely lunch with truly lovely people, I was still convinced: I didn't belong. I needed to prove myself.

Night after night, I walked into the studio between eight and nine o'clock to prepare for the overnight newscast. I'd sit next to Rob Nelson, my co-anchor and soon-to-be friend, in the work space that was adjacent to the studio. There we'd pore over the news of the day with our producers, preparing talking points.

After the late-night shows, we'd take our positions and deliver our version of the news. *World News Now* was a quirky, sometimes irreverent news broadcast, and we brainstormed ways to keep the attention of the late-night, early morning crowd. The insomniacs. The nursing mothers. The men and women taking third-shift coffee breaks. We went off script more than we stayed on, and we played to our strengths— Rob, the former partier turned respectable news anchor, and me, the long-time good girl becoming a somewhat less respectable news anchor. Whether or not it was funny I can't say, but we laughed. Maybe too much. And to this day I maintain the only reason we didn't get fired was because the executives who occupied the offices upstairs were asleep by the time we went on air.

World News Now was the perfect place to learn the craft of news anchoring, a place that allowed me to make the most of my personality. But that wasn't my only role at the station. After the show went off the air around five in the morning, I'd work on segments for upcoming shows, do voice-over work for other stories, and file reports. And twelve hours after arriving for my night shift, I'd leave the office, making my way home for a fitful bout of day-sleeping.

Night after night, as I walked into the studio, I saw the faces plastered on screens in the ABC News lobby: Diane Sawyer, Charlie Gibson, Robin Roberts, David Muir—all the people from that luncheon. They'd done what it took to achieve, to succeed, to prove they belonged in such a tough industry. And as their smiling faces watched me make my way to the elevator, I wanted nothing more than to see my face up there too.

Then I'd have earned my place.

Then the fear of failure would be a distant memory.

Then I'd be enough.

Right?

The need for approval—it was insatiable. So I said yes to every opportunity, every report, every assignment. *Good Morning America* began calling, asking me to file reports in the morning after my shift on *World News Now*. It might cost me a little sleep, but wasn't anything worth having worth sacrificing for? To achieve, didn't I need to continue stepping out of my comfort zone and into new opportunities? After all, this was my calling. Right?

Sleep suffered. Time with my family waned. Still, I was doing what it took, and the producers started to notice. Did I feel any less like an impostor, though? Not really. When I thought about it too long, I grew short of breath.

On a day like any other, I sat in my office trying to breathe, fingers tingling. What was I doing here? How had I been placed with such extraordinary journalists with amazing résumés? I locked the door, got on my knees, raised my hands to the sky, and begged for help.

"You brought me here, God. You're going to have to come through."

It was a quick prayer, followed by a quick amen. I picked myself up off the floor and decided to muscle through. If God had equipped me, maybe I could blast through this fear of not fitting in by working more. Surely success would help me feel better. Surely it would help me to not feel so much like an impostor. Wouldn't it?

Misalignment and the Fear of Being an Impostor

What is impostor syndrome? According to an article by Ellen Hendriksen in *Scientific American*,

> Impostor Syndrome is a pervasive feeling of self-doubt, insecurity, or fraudulence despite often overwhelming evidence to the contrary. It strikes smart, successful individuals. It often rears its head after an especially notable accomplishment, like admission to a prestigious university, public acclaim, winning an award, or earning a promotion.[1]

Put more simply, impostor syndrome is the manifestation of a very specific sort of fear—the fear of not fitting in.

We've all felt it at some point in our career. For some of us—maybe most of us—impostor syndrome follows us well into the latter years of our careers. It doesn't care how successful you are; impostor syndrome can still follow you. During the writing of this book, I spoke with Michael Strahan, the former New York Giants defensive end and current host of *Good Morning America*. I told him I so often feel like I don't fit in, and I asked whether he experienced the same sense. He laughed and asked, "Are you serious? I feel like that all the time."

Put more simply, impostor syndrome is the manifestation of a very specific sort of fear—the fear of not fitting in.

Michael Strahan suffers from impostor syndrome?

I suppose it makes sense that Strahan would. After all, after an incredibly successful career in the NFL, he'd had his own vocational shift. He moved into sports broadcasting, becoming an NFL analyst. After a few years as an analyst, he moved into daytime television, becoming the co-host of *Live! With Kelly and Michael*. Four years later, he became the weekday *GMA* co-host. His career had been a roller coaster of vocational moves. How had he stayed balanced through it all? He surrounded himself with good people who helped him stay centered, people like his business partner, Constance Schwartz-Morini.

See? Even the most successful among us find ourselves asking the same questions, especially when we step out of our comfort zones:

Will my bosses find out I really don't know what I'm doing?

Will my co-workers find out I'm winging it?

Will everyone in my field find out I'm a fraud?

These questions of belonging, of competency, maybe of fear, are not necessarily bad things. They can show us when we're unbalanced, when we're not trusting God with our vocational callings. In other words, they can show us when we're not focused on—and deeply rooted in—our faith callings.

Consider for a moment: If I'd had a firm grasp on my faith calling, would that sense of being an impostor have been so acute? Firmly rooted in my faith calling, wouldn't I have remembered that God had put me there for a particular season and particular reasons? Focused on my faith calling, I might have better understood that I wasn't meant to comfort myself by working harder, doing more. I was meant to feel the comfort of God as I found my fit in him, as I shared his love with the world around me. In that realization, wouldn't I have seen that I was exactly where God wanted me to be, with the people he wanted me around? Wouldn't all those impostor feelings have dissipated?

Remembering who we are in God—his beloved children—where he's placed us, and the people he's placed around us affects our decision-making and thought processes, and even reminds us not to worry in times of fear. But if we elevate our vocational calling above our faith calling, we're bound to become unrooted, maybe even uprooted. Our identity will be in what we do rather than who we are.

Consider the disciples, men who allowed their faith callings to direct their vocational callings. When they came face-to-face with Jesus, when they placed their faith in him, everything changed. But, it didn't change instantly.

God had equipped these men with certain gifts. But until they accepted their faith calling, those gifts had been misplaced. Even nonexistent, perhaps.

They trusted Jesus' teaching: "I am the vine; you are the branches. If you remain in me and I in you, you will bear much fruit" (John 15:5). Once they followed Christ, they drew all their strength, nourishment, and resources from the vine of faith calling, but it took some reorienting of their lives and vocations to get there.

Paul had misplaced his gift of leadership. He was slaughtering Christians because they threatened his belief system. He was a zealous Pharisee, defending his faith, defending the law. But after his conversion, Paul used that gift of leadership to defend his faith in the person of Jesus. At one time a murderer of Christians, Paul now became their fiercest advocate.

Still, Paul had to push through his guilt and accept God's grace, saying in 1 Corinthians 15:9–10, "I . . . do not even deserve to be called an apostle, because I persecuted the church of God. But by the grace of God I am what I am, and his grace to me was not without effect."

And Peter developed nonexistent gifts. He who had denied Jesus three times, who had sliced the ear of a Roman guard, who had a hot temper, left his fishing nets to become a preacher. He spoke to crowds of thousands, performing many miracles; he also endured persecution and ultimately suffered death.

Peter's transformation is reminiscent of Moses, who according to Exodus 4:10 was "slow of speech and tongue." Yet God asked Moses to speak dozens of times (I've seen no fewer than seventy times), including boldly proclaiming to Pharoah, the most powerful human in the known world, to "Let my people go" (Exodus 10:3).

When God calls you, he'll equip you. It becomes less about what you can bring to the table and more about being expectant that God will show up.

Having found their faith calling, these men embarked on lives of ministry. And when the hard days of persecution came, did they have second thoughts? Did they ever waver in their calling? Did they question whether or not they were good enough to be preachers and teachers? Were they concerned about being impostors?

Whatever their struggles, they remained anchored in both their faith and vocational callings—so much so that Paul and Peter were martyred.

Most of us aren't as clear in our vocational calling as the disciples were in theirs. And I'm guessing most of us won't die as martyrs. So often we lose sight of who we are and come to believe our vocation depends on our strength, our effort, and our abilities. We unroot our vocational calling from who we are in God and get all wrapped up in what we do, trying to find our identity in it. And when we suffer any kind of setback in it, the fear of being an impostor sets in. It's a fear that affects news anchors, lawyers, and even preachers.

God Does the Most Amazing Things, Even with Impostors

Weeks after my meeting with Robin (and the subsequent bodega snack run), I meet Bishop T. D. Jakes, pastor of The Potter's House church, at a hotel conference room in his hometown of Dallas, Texas. He is speaking at a conference and has agreed to an interview for the podcast between sessions.

Jakes is a successful man by any measure, pastoring 40,000 congregants. He has earned the title *Bishop* because he trains and oversees a number of younger ministers in various churches across the country. He has written more than forty-one books, including a *New York Times* bestselling entrepreneurial book, *Soar.* He is accomplished, and it's easy to see why. A large man, standing well over six feet tall and with a booming voice, he is an imposing figure. His fashion game is strong, and he carries that intangible quality leaders so often seem to embody, which demands respect. Still, there's nothing intimidating about him. There is something easy in the way he walks.

We waste no time and get straight to the interview. I catch up on Jakes's upbringing—raised in a West Virginia church, he made a profession of faith early. He shares how he knew God was calling him to preach while he was still in his teenage years. Still, he ran from it. Why? He was horrified, terrified. What's more, he had a speech impediment.

"I don't hear it now," I say.

"Sometimes it'll come out. . . . But I was born with a big gap in my teeth. And so I had a lisp growing up as a child, and it affected my speech and I went to speech therapists."

The speech impediment—it could have been the thing that kept Jakes from pressing into his vocational calling. And for a while, it did. He recalls how, in the middle of that season of running from God's call on his life, he was sitting on a barstool in a nightclub in West Virginia when a man approached him and said, "I had the weirdest dream about you, man. I dreamed you were preaching." But even a dream didn't break Jakes's will. How could God use Jakes, a boy with such limitations, a boy with a lisp, a boy with a "scuffed and scarred" history?

Jakes laughs as he remembers, then says, "God is full of oxymorons; he does some of the most amazing things with the most unlikely people."

Jakes eventually overcame his fears and made it into the ministry. He began shepherding a small church in West Virginia with just ten congregants—and eventually left with fifty families to begin The Potter's House in Dallas. It was a hard season, a season of poverty in which his family scraped by on public assistance. There were days when he and his wife sometimes skipped meals so his kids could eat. Even as The Potter's House grew faster than Jakes could have imagined, even as it exploded to more than 10,000 members in two years, Jakes was still pouring resources into the church. Still, he let neither the poverty nor the success go to his head. He wasn't distracted by either impostor syndrome or hero complexes.

How did he stay out of the ditches?

"I'm very much grounded in who I am as a person, and that's such a good thing," Jakes says. And who is he? A man carrying the treasure of faith in an earthen vessel, he replies, a sheep called to carry the truth of God out in a world of wolves.

We end the interview, and I thank Bishop Jakes for his time. As he walks back to the conference, I review my notes, considering what he'd just said. He had felt unworthy, that he didn't belong, that he had so many limitations, and still he'd pushed through the impostor syndrome and into his vocational calling. How? He was rooted into his faith calling. His purpose—to love God and love others—helped him navigate *what he did*.

Jakes and I had taken different approaches to dealing with the fear of impostor syndrome. At the beginning of my career, I'd had my own fears of inadequacy, but I faced those fears and pushed into the dream my mentors saw for me. I overcame the fear brought by external challenges too—the criticism, harassment, and even the marital issues I had caused through my own stupidity. I'd cultivated a desire bigger than my fear and had made the jump out of my comfort zone to New York City. But this move into those opportunities brought questions, challenges, and self-doubt. So what was the difference between Jakes and me? I wasn't as firmly rooted in my faith calling, in *who I was*.

In those early days at ABC, I was a professing Christian, one who attended church most Sundays. But was faith directing my decision-making? I certainly said so. Was I actively listening to the voice of God, though? Hardly. Was I in conversation with him about the pace? Nope. As a result, I felt like I didn't belong. So even though I wanted to slow down, though I wanted to spend more time with my family and friends, I didn't. Though I was a person of faith, my decisions weren't flowing from my faith. My decisions were driven by what others would think of me, fears that I wasn't good enough, worthy enough, or didn't belong. And so, to overcome these fears, I worked.

> In those years, my vocation had begun to define me. And this didn't lead to my finest moments.

And worked.

And worked.

If I could make it there, I could make it anywhere.

It's up to me. New York, New York.

In those years, my vocation had begun to define me. And this didn't lead to my finest moments.

The Beginning of the End

Two years into my stint at ABC, my work ethic (read: my insanity) had paid off. I was getting better interviews and better assignments, even if it meant I was sleeping less and spending less time with my family.

I was burning it at both ends, running on adrenaline. And in the middle of that very crazy season, John and I discovered we were pregnant with our third child, another boy. (Yes, we know what causes that.) And five months into that pregnancy, while still working like a crazy woman, I received some good news. I was up for promotion.

The executive team wanted to make me the co-host of the weekend edition of *Good Morning America*. What's more, I was asked to cover the 2014 World Cup in Brazil the following summer.

With my background in sports, covering the World Cup for a national network was a dream come true, though the timing was terrible. But how could I refuse? Didn't I need to prove I was a team player, that I was worthy of the bright lights and big stage? Didn't I need to prove I was worthy of the anchor position for *GMA Weekend?* And besides, if I pulled this off, wouldn't it help me make an even bigger name for myself? Maybe then I'd finally fit in.

I did some quick math, figured the baby would be around four months old by the time the assignment rolled around. There was no way in Hades I'd leave my baby behind, especially since I was dead set on nursing him just as I had my other two, but maybe I could bring him along. Maybe I could hire a nanny for the road. I could make it work. Couldn't I?

I emailed the producer, said I'd love to take the assignment on one condition: They had to let me take my newborn. They must have thought I was crazy, but they didn't balk. Instead, they agreed, and I began researching nannies for my upcoming trip to Brazil.

Landon was born on January 7, 2014, and months later, he attended his first World Cup soccer match. (John and I get the kids started on sports early in our house.) After landing in Brazil, after meeting the nanny who would turn out to be a godsend, after settling into the one-bedroom apartment where we'd make our home for the following month, I headed off to cover my first event.

That month was more difficult than I'd imagined. Because the World Cup isn't like the Olympics, because it wasn't located in one city but was spread out across Brazil—from Rio de Janeiro to Salvador to Brasilia to São Paulo—there were times I left Landon with the nanny for days on end. It was a blur of travel and interviewing and nursing and pumping, and though I wish I could say it was the time of my life, it wasn't. My sleep schedule was irregular. When I wasn't up in the middle of the night nursing a baby, I was traveling across the country to another venue. What's more, I was uncomfortable more days than not, because my feeding and pumping routine was less than regular. In fact, on a trip from a game to the airport, chest throbbing because I was so engorged, I knew I couldn't wait. I felt every bump in the road, every pothole, and I had to relieve some of the pressure. My producer, Emily Stanitz, was in the car, and I looked at her and said, "I'm sorry for what's about to happen." And then, right there in the back seat of the car, I attached myself to my portable breast pump and relieved the pressure. Needless to say, Emily and I have been close ever since.

But it wasn't just the lack of sleep and the mammary discomfort that made my World Cup experience difficult. I was plagued with guilt. I could have said no to the assignment and no one would have thought twice about it. I had a newborn, after all. But addicted to achievement, needing it to prove I fit in, that I'd earned the *GMA Weekend* co-anchor seat, I left John, Caroline, and JJ behind and carted my newborn five thousand miles from home. And was I really bonding with Landon as I traveled across Brazil? And had it been safe to take my baby to Rio—a dangerous city—and leave him with a stranger more days than not? Ummm . . . no. On both counts.

I wouldn't have said it at the time, but I'd lost sight of my faith calling; it had clouded my judgment. If you'd have asked, I would have told you I cared about family, friends, God, and church. My life choices were showing otherwise, though. My life choices were showing that I was finding my identity in *what I did* instead of *who I was*. I had reached the bottom. I was completely dependent on my addiction: achievement. It was the only thing that made me feel like I belonged.

CHAPTER 8

Trading One Identity for Another

There were things I didn't know in those early years in New York, at least not explicitly. I didn't appreciate the difference between my faith calling and my vocational calling, between who I was made to be and what I did. I didn't know that I was already enough for the God who loved me, that I didn't have to prove myself to him—or to anyone else, for that matter. What's more, I didn't recognize how my career was just the vehicle by which I'd show God's love to the world around me, and at the pace I was traveling, I never would have discovered this truth. I needed to slow down.

In the summer of 2014, I finally made it. Onto the wall, that is. A photo of the *GMA Weekend* team—including Dan Harris and me—hung in the lobby of the ABC News World Headquarters. Beside us hung photos of Diane, George, Robin, David, and so many of the incredible names in news. Didn't this mean I belonged? Shouldn't I feel that I fit? But as the weeks had passed, my need to achieve had only grown. I still felt the need to show I deserved my place on that screen. I wanted to prove I was worthy. I wanted to be a household name.

I was only weeks into my stint as the weekend co-anchor for *GMA*, and though I wasn't working the overnight shift, the schedule was just as brutal. I woke every weekend at 3:30 in the morning and hopped into the car the studio provided for those of us who were early risers, often sans makeup and still in my pajamas. There were mornings I was so haggard, security had to do a double take at my badge and face. This is what the grind does to a woman—makes her often unrecognizable to others, sometimes to herself.

Past security, I'd meet the studio team before the five o'clock hour. We'd cover stories and review scripts while Camille Zola, my makeup artist, and Christine Healey, my hair stylist, worked legitimate miracles to get me camera ready. By seven o'clock, I was put together and on the air with Dan Harris, Sara Haines, Ron Claiborne, and Rob Marciano, my weekend *GMA* family.

For the most part, my role at *GMA Weekend* was the same as at *World News Now*. Narrate the stories. Offer commentary. Create an inviting space for the early weekend risers who welcomed me into their homes. And when our last show wrapped on Sunday, I'd go home, catch up on sleep, and prepare for the upcoming week, for filing reports for the weekday editions of *GMA*, *World News Tonight*, and *Nightline*. Some days I'd fill in for one of the co-anchors on the weekday edition of *GMA*. My days were packed with research, writing, and reporting. And on the weekend, it was back to the 3:30 a.m. wakeup call. I was coming and going, barely sleeping as I chased my own ego, my "calling." And though I didn't notice, it started taking a physical toll on me.

After a particularly hectic workweek, I slogged down to the car on a Sunday morning and made my way to the studio. I slept through the short trip, then rolled out of the car and made my way into the building, disheveled. In my pajamas at the guard station, I rifled through my purse, searching for my ID. Had I left it on the counter? I apologized and told him I didn't have my ID, but that I was reporting for my on-air duties. He was unconvinced. In fact, he wouldn't clear me. I pointed at the photo on the lobby wall, gave him details only I would know. Still, he wasn't budging. While the guard kept a wary eye on me, Walt Berry, a *GMA* stagehand, happened to walk into the lobby, and he noticed the standoff. He came to the guard stand and vouched for me. "It's her," he said, a relief since he might have exercised the opportunity to pull a practical joke. With that, the guard let me in.

Identity—had I let it go?

When I wasn't on the air or producing reports, I filled in for other morning shows, including the daytime women's talk show *The View*. I suppose I wasn't terrible, because in the summer of 2015, the network asked whether I'd consider taking a full-time co-host role on the show while continuing to co-anchor *GMA Weekend*. It would be a demanding workload, the network said, but they'd try to get me a day off each week. One day? What day? They couldn't say, which should have been a red flag. It wasn't, though. And though I could have forced the issue, though I could have asked them to set a day, I didn't. It was another chance to move up the ladder, another opportunity to play with the big boys (or girls, as it were). And though it'd take me away from John and the kids a little more, every career requires sacrifice. After all, I was walking in my vocational calling, right?

Weeks after accepting the position, on a Saturday morning, I was on-set with the team, and at the close of the show, Sara Haines announced my new role with *The View*. I assured our weekend audience

I wasn't going anywhere, that I could handle multiple roles. Then I turned to a little levity.

"What we thought was scientifically and anatomically impossible? Nope. I'm going to be in two places at once," I said.

Sara chimed in, laughing. "Paula has given up sleep in the name of her fans."

"Don't worry, I'll be taking some days off here and there." I said this as if trying to convince myself.

"No, you won't," said Ron Claiborne, the news reader, laughing with Sara and me.

Tom Llamas, who was filling in for Dan Harris that week, wasn't laughing. "Seven days a week. Wow."

Looking back, we all knew it—I was crazy, over-working, sacrificing everything for the next big move. And yet we made jokes about it, laughed about it. After all, wasn't I doing what I wanted to do? Wasn't I making a name for myself, forging my own identity?

My assignment on *The View* was simple. Be the neutral journalist, my bosses said. Stay in the center, avoid showing my political or religious cards. I was still a journalist, after all, filing reports and conducting interviews for other shows on the network, and I needed to maintain a sense of impartiality. The only problem? I sat in the seat of Elisabeth Hasselbeck, an outspoken and conservative Christian who'd been no stranger to sharing her opinion. And so, by the optics alone, viewers and co-hosts alike must have thought I'd been inserted into the lineup to carry her torch. So it should come as no surprise that the women on the show expected me to mix it up a little more, to share my own opinions on issues of faith and politics. And as the weeks passed, I began to realize there was a growing disconnect between my

> Looking back, we all knew it—I was crazy, overworking, sacrificing everything for the next big move. And yet we laughed about it.

amazing co-hosts (all of whom I still love) and me. The network had a set of expectations. My co-hosts had another set of expectations. I was caught in the middle and unsure of how to square the two.

I should have been clearer with my co-hosts about my assignment, my position. I should have asked for some intervention from the network executives. I didn't do either. And so, show after show, the tension mounted. Co-hosts were agitated as I avoided taking sides during interviews, discussions of current events, and political debates. I grew agitated—as much with myself as with anyone else—as I tried to avoid the minefields of opinion, knowing that if I slipped, if I seemed to take one side or the other, I might kill my news career as an impartial reporter. After all, impartiality was the stock-in-trade, the calling card of any respectable journalist.

After each taping of *The View*, I returned to my dressing room fully aware that I was the odd woman out. And because I had such a good team with such good chemistry on the weekend edition of *GMA*, I recognized that the chemistry at *The View* was off. What was worse, it was my own fault, at least in part.

Had I ever prayed about accepting the job? No.

Had I been clear enough about my parameters, about the expectations? Nope.

Had I simply taken the position because it represented another feather in my cap? No doubt.

Was my identity so wrapped up in my career that I'd do anything and everything to advance it? Sure enough.

I considered my potential failure on *The View*, and that's when the fear came. In fact, the fear seemed to metastasize, to shapeshift, to turn into something more like a reality. I didn't wonder whether I was a failure; I knew I was. But in that fear, in that knowledge, I did what I'd always done. I doubled down and put in as many hours as I could, convinced achievement and accomplishment might push back the growing sense of failure and the accompanying fears—the fear that

I didn't deserve my job; fear that I was an impostor; fear that I'd be canned and forgotten. I worked so much, in fact, that I didn't worry about that pie-in-the-sky day off I'd been promised.

Seven days a week.

Around the clock.

Twenty-one-day stretches without a break.

This was my life.

Though the situation on *The View* was becoming more and more untenable, other areas of my career were showing promise. The weekend edition of *GMA* was still a sweet spot, and because I hadn't been shy about my faith, I started receiving faith-oriented assignments, namely stories of faith under fire. In September 2015, I flew to Kentucky, where I interviewed Kim Davis, the controversial clerk of Rowan County who defied a federal court order and refused to issue marriage licenses to same-sex couples, saying it violated her Christian principles. In March 2016, I interviewed the Duggar siblings of *19 Kids and Counting*, a popular reality television show that highlighted a large Christian family from Arkansas, who had come under fire after allegations surfaced that Josh Duggar, one of the brothers, had molested five under-aged girls, including four of his sisters, when he was a teenager.

> I considered my potential failure on The View, and that's when the fear came. In fact, the fear seemed to metastasize, to shapeshift, to turn into something more like a reality. I didn't wonder whether I was a failure; I knew I was.

As one year turned to another, John came to me and told me the jobs were taking a toll. We needed a break, he said. A time to reconnect. But how? John was now managing one of the top commercial real estate agencies in NYC, Marcus & Millichap. His schedule allowed for weekend travel, but my primary duty continued to be hosting the weekend edition of *GMA*, and since I never knew exactly when my day off during the week would be, it was impossible to sync our schedules.

We were in an endless, mindless loop—wake, work, sleep, rinse, repeat. The lights of love were burning dim while the tensions were reigniting. And this is what led to my first lunch meeting, the one where I tried to quit my co-anchoring positions on *GMA* weekend and *The View*. It was the meeting where the well-meaning executive convinced me I was crazy to step away. We reached a compromise over that lunch. I'd scale back, move to one day a week on *The View*, and continue to anchor *GMA Weekend*. It would keep me relevant, in the mix. It would let me spend a little more time with my family. And though I knew it was the right thing, still I wondered.

What will people think when they find out?

Will they think I was forced out?

Will they think I'm a failure?

Truth is, it didn't matter if others thought I was a failure. I was already convinced I was.

Calling—It's Bigger than the Job You Do

From the earliest age, I internalized the primary messages society and the church sent about calling: *Calling* and *career* are synonymous. Just as priests and pastors were "called to the ministry," my dad was called to be an engineer. I heard teachers describe their classroom as their calling, and doctors say they were called to work in medicine. Mothers said their primary calling was to raise children. Everyone had a calling, and that calling was *what they did.*

As I grew older, I heard preacher after preacher speak about how God "called us to the workplace." Sure, some of my pastors and priests were a little more nuanced in the ways they discussed calling, but for whatever reason, the subtleties didn't stick. Even today, as I hear Christian leaders speak about our callings, there is a stunning lack of both nuance and specificity. So often, it is simply implied that our calling is what we do from nine to five. Our calling is our career.

As followers of Christ, we need to root into a different truth. Our primary calling is not our vocation. It is not our jobs. Our primary calling is singular: *Love God with all your heart, soul, mind, and strength, and love your neighbor as yourself* (see Mark 12:30–31). In other words, love God and love people. According to Jesus, these are the two greatest commands. And if we're not clear about our primary calling, our faith calling, if we conflate calling with our career, we're destined to promote our own agendas, our own careers, all the while losing sight of God and others.

Jesus is the perfect embodiment of his own teaching. In the gospel of John, we find him in the city of Jerusalem just days before his death. After predicting his death, he turns to the disciples and says,

> Even though I am torn within, and my soul is in turmoil, I will not ask the Father to rescue me from this hour of trial. For I have come to fulfill my purpose—*to offer myself to God*. So, Father, bring glory to your name!
>
> John 12:27–28 TPT

Jesus knew his purpose, his faith calling—to love God and love people. How did he express that love? Through what he did, through sacrificing himself for all mankind. And if he had seated his identity in any other vocation—his life as a carpenter, rabbi, or leader of men—wouldn't he have done anything to avoid that death for the sake of his vocation?

If we conflate calling with our career, we're destined to promote our own agendas, our own careers, while losing sight of God and others.

Throughout the rest of the New Testament, we see just how Peter and Paul live into their primary calling to love God and love people through preaching, pastoring, and writing letters to the early church.

The notion of calling is woven throughout their writing, in fact. They discuss the call of all followers of Christ, but in no instance do they write or even imply that calling and vocation are synonymous. Instead, they write of the calling to obey Jesus' teachings (2 Timothy 1:9; 1 Peter 1:5–16), to follow his purposes (Romans 8:28), and to persevere in the love of God, even when persecuted (Philippians 3:14; 1 Peter 2:21; and 1 Peter 3:9). If there's any implication in their writings, it's that our primary calling is to love God and love people, all the way to the end.

As Christians, it's time to have a much bigger, more nuanced conversation about calling. Calling isn't just about your vocation. It's more holistic. It's not what you do, it's who you've been created to be—a follower of the living God who shares his love with a hurting world. And when we come to understand this truth, we see our true identity—we are representatives of the living, loving God. I didn't fully appreciate this truth in the first half of my career. I poured myself into my career, made it my life, my identity, and in that, a subtle twisting happened. What was that twisting?

I believed this: The God who had called me *to be a reporter* would equip me *to be a reporter.*

Instead of believing this: The God who'd called me *to love God and love people* would equip me *to express that love through my vocation, whatever that vocation happened to be.*

When God calls you, he will always equip you, but he equips you to an identity rooted in your faith calling, not in your career. And sure, part of that equipping might be the skills, training, and talent needed to succeed in your vocational calling so that you can carry his love to others in that field. But that's not all. God also equips you with a brain. He'll equip you with common sense and the ability to discern when you're falling out of balance, when you're going so fast you've lost sight of what matters. And if you don't use that brain? He'll figure out a way to slow you down. I learned that the hard way.

What Didn't Kill Me Only Made Me Work Harder

A few days after that lunch with the executive, after my decision to scale back, I was scheduled to travel to Cleveland for the Republican National Convention. Knowing the news of my departure might break while I was out of town, and not wanting to blindside Whoopi Goldberg or the crew while I was away, I visited her in her office and told her I'd decided to step back.

She asked if they were going to lose me.

"Not a chance. I'll still be here part time, I just need to step back a little," I replied.

She nodded. Understood. Wished me luck in Cleveland.

A day later I stood on the floor of the convention, preparing to interview political operatives, movers and shakers, and state delegates. And that's when I got the call. It was Julie Townsend, head of ABC's public relations team. She told me an article had hit *Page Six*. The headline: "Paula Faris is getting axed from 'The View.'"

I thanked her, hung up, then navigated to the *Page Six* website. I scanned the article:

> "ABC News was hoping [Paula] would bring a more conservative perspective to the show because she's a conservative Christian. But she doesn't own her opinions and the audience never connects with anyone who's pretending," a source told us.[1]

The article went on to say that market research had found me unlikable. To add insult to injury, also according to the unnamed source,

> Whoopi Goldberg is "elated about this. She has never been a fan of Paula's. The tension on air has been so thick, you could cut it with a knife. Whoopi never misses an opportunity to bite her head off over any given topic."[2]

The truth was there—just buried six paragraphs down. An unnamed insider was quoted as saying that I was a journalist, that my job was to be objective. "She was never brought to the table to have the same role as Joy Behar," the insider said.

My worst fears had come to life. I'd be seen as a failure, someone who couldn't hack it on *The View*. And as the weight of the article spread across my shoulders, as it settled in the pit of my stomach, tears streamed down my face. My producer turned to me and asked me what was wrong, but I just wiped my eyes and told her my allergies were killing me. Did she buy it? I doubt it. When she read the headlines, she'd know.

The next morning I was reporting live from the convention floor for *The View*. Earpiece in, I heard Whoopi's voice, speaking live to the studio audience and the viewers watching at home.

"We sent Paula out into the lions' den."

You can say that again.

"She's right out there in the middle of all the action at the Republican National Convention. She's joining us now, live from Cleveland."

A smile plastered across my face, I waved at the cameras with both hands. But the truth is, I don't remember it. In fact, I don't remember anything about that field report. I was in shock. Blank. Tingling. When I watch that footage now, I can see it on my face, the expression of having suffered an identity wound hidden just beneath the surface of my smile.

> My worst fears had come to life. I'd be seen as a failure, someone who couldn't hack it on The View.

I muscled my way through the rest of the convention and cried myself all the way back to New York. A week passed. Then another. There was so much speculation about my career, what had happened, whether I was being fired. And then the British tabloid *The Daily Mail* piled on. The wordy headline read, "Exclusive: 'This is a bunch of bull—it's

Whoopi's doing.' The View host Paula Faris is cut to one day a week and blames nemesis Goldberg in dressing room meltdown." (As an aside, what kind of headline is that?) It was an article meant to do one thing: burn down a reputation. It opened,

> Forget the Bible verse that says: "Vengeance is mine, I will repay, says the Lord". The devout-Christian co-host of The View Paula Faris is seeing red and vowing to get revenge on the show's moderator Whoopi Goldberg.[3]

The writer (whom I *refuse* to call a journalist) spun a fantastical tale about how I'd been told I was being cut in my dressing room, how I'd lost my cool and blamed Whoopi. And though the article wasn't true, though I hadn't had a dressing-room meltdown and hadn't blamed Whoopi for any of it, none of that mattered. The tabloids had set the narrative. The politics of journalism were spinning against me.

I had put all my eggs in the basket of my career. I'd given so much for it, had wrapped my identity up in it. But all I'd proven was that I couldn't hack it. All I'd proven is that I wasn't good enough. At least that's what I had thought then, and as that thought set in, I only knew one way to try to fix it: I'd work harder. I'd work more. I would prove I belonged. I would prove I was worthy of my career.

CHAPTER 9

How Martha Becomes Mary

I've learned a thing or two through my years of faith. Among them, I've learned that when we lose sight of our purpose, our identity, our faith calling, God will do his absolute best to get our attention. He'll use whatever it takes, even failure and pain. And that's how he got my attention.

In the wake of *The View* debacle, I kept hustling, and in the summer of 2017, all my hustling paid off. The year before, I'd met Sean Spicer at the Republican National Convention (RNC). Spicer was the communications director for the RNC, and during my brief stint in Cleveland, I developed a professional rapport with him. He'd gone on to become President Donald Trump's press secretary for the tumultuous first six months of the administration, and though I wasn't a White House press correspondent (jobs that belong to Chief White House Correspondent Jon Karl and Senior White House Correspondent Cecilia Vega, both of whom I love), Spicer and I had kept in touch. So when he resigned in August 2017, I reached out to him and asked if he'd give me an exclusive interview. He agreed. It would be his first network interview since he left the White House.

Things were looking up professionally. Scaling back at *The View* had been good for me, though I was still hitting it hard at the network. But it seemed things were shifting personally too. Weeks earlier, John and I discovered I was pregnant. As it turned out, the day before the interview with Spicer, I was scheduled for my nine-week ultrasound appointment. Although my schedule was hectic and I had a strategic prep session for the Spicer interview on the same day, I refused to reschedule this appointment. After all, this was the day we'd hear the heartbeat, the day we'd have our first interaction with our newest little one.

John, who continued to move up the chain at Marcus & Millichap, took an extra hour off and came with me to the doctor's office. In the exam room, he held my hand as the technician smeared goop on my belly and moved the wand back and forth over the spot where the baby should be. A minute passed. Maybe another. She left the room, then returned with the doctor, who wore a blank expression. The technician waved the wand over my belly again, then the doctor dropped the news like a ton of bricks.

"There's no heartbeat," she said. "We'll need to run some blood work and run a few tests. Do you have time today?"

Was that a serious question? Did I have time for my baby?

The doctor left the room as something like grief settled in. I turned to John, told him he should go back to work. There was nothing he could do to help me, and I had a strategy call for the Spicer interview

I'd have to take while the docs ran the labs. He'd be happy to stay with me, he said, but I assured him I was fine and shooed him out. He kissed me and told me to call him if I got any news. As soon as he was out of the room, I buried my face in my hands and cried.

I gathered my emotions just before I heard a knock at the door. It was a nurse, who ushered me to another room for the labs. As I was sitting in a chair, with needles in my arms, my phone rang. It was my conference call for the Spicer interview. I apologized, told them I had poor cell reception, which is why I hadn't called in yet. Did they buy the excuse? I didn't know, but we launched into the call as the nurse beside me busied herself, flittering around me with needles and monitors and a blood pressure cuff.

As she drew blood, the team and I recalled Spicer's claims that President Trump's inauguration was the most attended inauguration in history, despite photographic evidence to the contrary. While the nurse measured my heart rate, we discussed the ways Spicer had sparred with the press, often castigating reporters and storming out of the room. When the nurse slipped the blood pressure cuff on my arm, I asked the researchers whether they could get me video of his appearance on the Emmy Awards just days before. (Some believe he'd made an appearance on the television awards show in an effort to repair his image, and I wanted to ask him whether that was true.) I laughed at a joke someone made about comedian Melissa McCarthy's portrayal of Spicer on *Saturday Night Live*, even as the nurse worked to determine whether I'd lost my baby.

The nurse finished her data gathering, I wrapped up my call, and the doctor returned to the room. "You'll need to come back in a week for another ultrasound. We'll call you soon with the results from the blood work," she said, then added, "Take it easy for the next couple of days. Okay?"

Sure thing, doc.

And as I walked out of the office, as the worst news hung over my head in the midst of a career high, nothing seemed right. I needed to slow down, to feel the grief, but where was the time? So I did what I was paid to do. I pushed through the unrelenting waves of disappointment and threw myself into the work. Hours later, I boarded a train to D.C., so I could get that interview with Sean Spicer.

The next day, I put on my most professional face and walked into the interview with Spicer, not knowing if my baby was still alive. I did my job, launched into what should have been a career-making interview. We spoke about the inauguration, how Spicer had claimed it was the largest attended in history. He admitted to wishing he'd had more of the evidence and been more specific. Spicer went on, revealing that the president could be difficult to work with. He then admitted he hadn't used careful language around the White House travel ban that was put in place early in the administration, a travel ban that had prevented refugees and asylum seekers from certain (mostly Middle Eastern) countries from receiving safe passage to the United States. At the end of the interview, I asked whether he had any regrets about his combative relationship with the press corp. He did, he said, and where he'd made mistakes, he'd tried to own them. As for a blanket apology for his time at the White House?

I put on my most professional face and walked into the interview with Sean Spicer, not knowing if my baby was still alive.

"That's not happening," he said.

The interview lasted almost an hour, but it was a blur. Focused as I tried to be, I couldn't shake the concern for my baby. How could these two surreal events be converging? My career high, my personal low.

We wrapped the interview, and it ran the following day on *GMA*. It was a career-making moment, and my colleagues congratulated me. I'd pulled one off for the team, and by all accounts, I did it in fine fashion. But what does success do for you in the middle of a miscarriage?

Days after the interview, I returned to the doctor. They repeated the ultrasound, and this time confirmed what I already knew. I'd lost the baby. I was far enough along that I'd need to take a pill to "clean out," the doctor said. She gave me a vaginal suppository and sent me home, telling me I should expect to feel better in a few days. Instead of going home, though, I went back to work, and that's where I started bleeding. Light bleeding became moderate bleeding. Moderate bleeding turned to heavy bleeding. A day after taking the pill, I was all-out hemorrhaging.

Three days later, I went back to my doctor, nearly passing out in the reception area. They examined me and discovered I hadn't passed the baby. In fact, I'd developed a uterine infection. It was time for an emergency D&C (dilation and curettage), a procedure to strip the fetal tissue from my womb. I don't remember much about the D&C, except that it was horrifying, even if necessary. The procedure finally complete, they pumped me full of antibiotics and sent me on my way.

I didn't get to bed until 11:00 that night, and by 3:30 a.m. I was walking out the door to catch my ride to the studio. Should I have gone to work the next morning? Nope. Could I have gone to the producers and told them I needed some time off to heal physically and emotionally? Without a question. Should I have taken the time to seek spiritual comfort from God? Um . . . duh. If I took time off, though, the emotions would catch up with me, maybe remind me that even my body was a failure. Work—it was the only thing that could numb me to the emotions pressing in.

Work, work, work. I could work my way through the pain. I could work my way through anything. Work could distract me from the fear, the emotion. Work—it's such a useful coping mechanism.

When Our Career Becomes Everything

Ah, work—it was my drug of choice. It's something I could control, something that brought me a sense of worth. But rooted in my vocational calling as I was, deriving so much pleasure from it, I never asked whether God was actually pleased with the way I was working. I never stopped to ask *why* God brought me into the field of journalism. And if I had my guess, most of you don't know the *why* of your vocational calling either.

According to a 2014 Gallup poll of more than one thousand participants, over 55 percent of American workers say they gain their sense of identity from their job, and among college graduates, the number is even higher, at 70 percent.[1] But you don't need a Gallup poll to tell you that American workers highly identify with their careers. Just consider the question most often asked when you meet someone new: *What do you do for a living?* We don't ask, *Why do you do what you do?* Much less, *What is the purpose of your life?*

We weren't made to wrap up so much of our identity in what we do, but we do. And because so much of our identity is seated in our occupation, many of us leverage everything to advance that career. We make wonky decisions, such as going to work less than five hours after an emergency D&C. We miss the best things that are right in front of our faces, things like time with God, family, and friends, and all because we've misplaced our identity.

I missed opportunities to experience God's comfort, to share his love with my family, friends, and co-workers. And although I feel awful about that fact, I'm not the only one. In fact, people have been making this mistake since the beginning of time, even some of Jesus' closest friends.

In Luke chapter 10, Jesus and his disciples stopped at the house of Mary and Martha, friends of Jesus and the disciples. While Jesus rested from his journey, Martha busied herself making preparations for her guests. Mary, on the other hand, sat at Jesus' feet, listening to him. Maybe he was teaching. Maybe he was sharing stories of his travels. Maybe he was telling "A rabbi, a tax collector, and a Roman walked into a bar" jokes. Whatever the case, Luke records that Martha was so busy *doing* that she couldn't simply *be* in the presence of Jesus. And as her frustration grew, she became demanding. (For the record, I wish I were a Mary, but I'm definitely a Martha.)

"Lord, don't you care that my sister has left me to do the work by myself? Tell her to help me!" Martha said (v. 40).

Jesus didn't bend to Martha's demands, though. (Don't we all find ourselves demanding things of God?) Instead, Jesus addressed her work anxiety with great love:

> "Martha, Martha," the Lord answered, "you are worried and upset about many things, but few things are needed—or indeed only one. Mary has chosen what is better, and it will not be taken away from her."
>
> Luke 10:41–42

Jesus was clear. Our worth doesn't come from our busyness, from all the things we do, not even the things we do for Jesus. Jesus is more concerned about whether we are loving him with our whole heart, mind, soul, and strength. That's where he wants us to find our worth, our identity. And when we're rooted in that identity, we can share the truth of God's love with the world around us. But when we lose sight of this truth, when we find our identity in what we do, we'll find ourselves mired in anxiety, fear, and worry, just as Martha did.

A word of caution, though. Don't hear what I'm not saying. I'm not saying that what you *do* doesn't matter. It's true that in certain seasons, God gives us specific tasks, particular jobs, and unique vocational callings. But those vocational callings aren't meant for our own praise, honor, or glory. They're not meant to be used as a way to get praise or attention, even from Jesus. What is the purpose of our work then? To take the love and light we've received from Christ and bring it to the world. How do I know? Jesus told us as much in his Sermon on the Mount. Recall the passage Jan Jeffcoat referenced:

You are the light of the world. A town built on a hill cannot be hidden. Neither do people light a lamp and put it under a bowl. Instead they put it on its stand, and it gives light to everyone in the house. In the same way, let your light shine before others, that they may see your good deeds and glorify your Father in heaven.

Matthew 5:14–16

See? We haven't been sent into the world to make much of our own names. We've been sent so we might make much of the light and love of God. But if we're going to do this, we have to spend time with him, to be lit up by him. We have to root our identities in him and his love.

What is the purpose of our work then? To take the love and light we've received from Christ and bring it to the world.

I never made it my primary aim to love God and love others through my vocational calling to broadcasting. I was too enamored with my own name, with making my way into the spotlight. I was too focused on climbing the next rung on the ladder. I set my sights on what I was doing with little regard to who I was supposed to be doing it for. And focused on myself as I was, I wasn't able to see God at work in the world around me, much less see the ways he was calling me to share his love. I didn't take the time to recognize those in my world who might need the love of God—at least, not until God made it plain in the most unlikely way: through a political rally.

The Beginning of an Epiphany

Just months after the miscarriage, I tracked down another exclusive lead. I'd spoken with the handlers for Roy Moore, the embattled senatorial candidate from Alabama who was no stranger to controversy. Twice named the chief justice of the Supreme Court of Alabama, he'd been twice removed. In 2003, he was stripped of his title after refusing a federal court order to remove a monument of the Ten Commandments from the Alabama Judicial Building. In 2016 Moore, a staunch opponent of same-sex marriage who'd once said that "homosexual conduct should be illegal," was suspended for defying the United States Supreme Court's ruling overturning bans on same-sex marriage. (Moore would later resign from the state's highest court.) In the summer of 2017 he was running for the Senate seat vacated when Alabama Senator Jeff Sessions accepted the position as the United States Attorney General under President Trump. But controversy had caught up with him again.

During the election, multiple women came forward, accusing Moore of sexual misconduct. Two alleged he sexually assaulted them when they were minors and Moore was in his mid-thirties. Others came forward claiming Moore made unwanted advances. The story took on a life of its own, and as the allegations piled on during the middle of the special election, the network asked me to try to get an exclusive interview. After all, this was right in my lane, the place where faith and politics collided. So with the help of my producers, I tracked down Moore's handlers and got them on the phone. There was a rally the next day, they said, and if I could make it, I might have a shot at speaking with Moore.

Getting to rural Alabama isn't easy, especially when you show up at LaGuardia Airport without your driver's license. But as I stepped from my cab, reaching for my credit card to pay the driver, I realized that's exactly what I'd done. Concerned I might miss the exclusive, that I might disappoint my bosses (and then I'd certainly be a disappointment), I hopped back in the cab and called my producer, Jaclyn Hart, to see whether they could find a flight that got me into Alabama in time for the interview. She found a flight out of Westchester County Airport, just twenty minutes from my house, and booked it. I told the cab driver to step on it, and after we stopped at the house for my license, he sped to the airport, cutting through traffic like only a New York cabbie could. I arrived with minutes to spare, running up to the gate just before they locked the doors. I'd made it. Maybe God was intervening.

I arrived at the small airport in Alabama and met Michael Del Moro, the ABC News booker, for the Moore interview. He directed the driver to a good old-fashioned American chain restaurant and told me we'd be meeting with the teetotaling Moore team before the rally. We could make our case for the exclusive interview there, and over the kind of Alabama sweet tea that makes your teeth hurt, that's exactly what we did. Our contact listened and nodded along but didn't make any promises. Things looked promising, though, and if I played my cards right, I might get the most-talked-about interview of the current news cycle.

Michael and I made our way to the venue, a rural Baptist church where Moore was delivering his speech. We were ushered to the annex— an unfinished gym with folding chairs—and I sat with the producer and cameraman in the back with the rest of the media. The major networks had come for the rally; I suspected they were doing their best to get an exclusive too. But had they had sweet tea with the Moore camp before the rally? I doubted it. I had the inside track.

Before Moore took the stage, a preacher stood to make the introduction. He delivered a sort of miniature sermon, one in which he denounced and openly mocked the gay community. "The L-G-B-T-Q-X-Y-Z . . . I can't even keep up with the letters," he said, drawing laughs and cheers from the crowd. Then he continued to connect them with the ills of American society. He railed against the Democrats as well, saying they'd created false accusations against Moore. He singled out the media, implied we didn't tell the truth. (As if all media are the same.) He claimed the country had gone off the moral rails, that we needed more men of God in it. Religious liberties were at stake, he said, and if we were going to preserve those religious liberties, we needed men like Moore at the helm of our country.

The preacher drew his sermon to a close and introduced Judge Roy Moore as the crowd whooped and clapped. The judge took the stage, and he spoke with a different sort of cadence than I'd become accustomed to on the campaign trail. He didn't so much sound like a politician as a preacher. It was the kind of speech I expected from Moore, though, one in which he discussed what he espoused as conservative Christian values. He was a committed Christian, a committed husband. He spoke about the erosion of morality in America also, and though he intimated he didn't have any problem with the LGBTQ community, he didn't do anything to put out the fire the preacher started. And as the scene unfolded, I could sense just how sad and angry Michael, the man sitting next to me, an openly gay man who was also a professing Christian, was becoming.

You can disagree with people and still do it with love, especially if everything flows from your faith calling to love God and love people.

The rally ended, and Moore's people said they'd be in touch regarding an interview down the road (an interview that would never materialize). As Michael and I headed back to the airport, I considered the evening. The preacher and Moore had whipped the crowd into a frenzy, but had he considered there might be someone in the room who was gay? Had he considered he might be compounding hurt and harm and reinforcing stereotypes of Christian hate, all for the sake of a Senate seat? Had he stopped for a moment to consider using his platform, his vocational calling as a candidate for public office to share the love of God with those in the room? Even people he might disagree with? Even the media?

It's my opinion that you can actually stand for certain things, certain positions, and still do it with love. In fact, you can disagree with people and still do it with love, especially if everything flows from your faith calling to love God and love people. Had the preacher and Moore done that?

Michael knew I was a professing Christian, and though he knew what he was getting into, I couldn't let Moore's brand of stumping go without rebuttal. I turned to him in the car and said, "You know we're not all that way, right?" He smiled and said he knew as much. It had been a jarring experience, though, one that had opened his eyes to how tied together anti-LGBTQ and pro-God rhetoric was in certain parts of the country. I told him I was sorry, told him God loved him. He knew, he said, but he thanked me anyway.

That was it. A simple comment. A simple thank-you. And then we moved on. But still, it was the beginning of the epiphany. Although I couldn't have said it at the time, I had come to a crossroads, a sort of intersection. I was beginning to see the two ways we can go about our vocational callings. We can hustle and strive and do, climbing the ladder without regard for those around us. We can go about our work in our own strength and power, hoping to make a name for ourselves. We can run at such a pace that we forget our own identity (and our IDs) and forget those in the world around us. Or we can take a different approach. We can use our vocational callings as a way to share the love of God with those around us. And although I'd found a way to do this at the Roy Moore rally, I didn't make it a daily practice. Still, a seed of something was growing. Maybe it was the seed of the purpose behind my vocational calling.

Maybe you sense you're out of balance, doing so much that you haven't taken time to rest, to sit with God and experience his love. Maybe you haven't asked him to show you the *why* behind your vocational calling. Maybe you haven't been intentional about shining your light in the world so that others might come to glorify God. If that's you, pay attention: If you're moving too fast to slow down and root yourself in your faith calling, you're moving too fast. If you don't slow down, rest assured, God will slow you down. That's what he would do for me after the Roy Moore rally. In fact, though I didn't know it, he was already doing it. The year of hell was upon me.

It was the year God would finally get my attention.

CHAPTER 10

The Year of Hell, the Year of Waking Up

It was the kind of New York morning that can be unsettling—a crisp autumn day, the sky still cobalt blue above Wall Street. I was standing outside the New York Stock Exchange building in Lower Manhattan with a camera crew ready. The stock market had been on a historic bull run, and I'd been sent by *GMA* to report on the seemingly endless upswing.

The sun began to rise over 11 Wall Street, and an eerie, Hitchcockian glow settled in. The crew gave me the signal—ten seconds until we went live. I stared into the camera, preparing myself to deliver my report as I'd done thousands of times, but just before the studio threw to me, something smashed into the back of my head. Then . . .

What the [insert expletive I'm not super proud I said]?!

Something like a ball struck me on the back of my head, just behind my right ear, and I doubled over in pain. Everything went some shade of gray, and tiny stars sparkled everywhere. I reached for the spot where I'd been hit. It was wet, and there were bits of whatever the exploded projectile was in my hair. The cameraman was squatting, asking me to look him in the eyes. At least I think remember that much. I'm less clear on what happened after, except that someone must have driven me to the emergency room. I have some vague memory of a doctor in blue scrubs saying I had a concussion. The next clear memory I have is of lying on the couch in my living room.

An average Wednesday had become a blur of activity. But it wasn't until the next day that I pieced together what had happened. I dragged myself to the office, head still throbbing and vision still blurred, and a producer dropped in. The camera crew had found pieces of an apple at the scene, he said. They'd called the police to report the incident, and New York City's finest had found street-level surveillance tapes, which added a little color. Two teenagers had been running toward a subway entrance, and as they descended the stairs, one of them launched an apple in my direction. The officers estimated the fruit was traveling somewhere around sixty miles per hour when it hit me in the head. Another inch to the right, it would have shattered the right side of my face.

I'd been assaulted with an apple in the Big Apple. Could my life be any *weirder*?

I muddled through the rest of that day. It felt as if I were looking through a piece of foggy cellophane, and my recall of simple things— names, words, the news stories of the week—was slow. Still, I wouldn't miss a day at the office, convinced I could muscle through anything, even apple-sault. Besides, I wasn't scheduled to be on air. I could hole up in the office until I snapped out of the fog. No one would even notice if I was a little out of it.

Friday rolled around, and the symptoms still lingered. There was work to do though. I was scheduled to host *The View*, and I wasn't going to let a little thing like a concussion stop me. I was nauseated, off balance, and still not clear-headed, but I could fake my way through. At least that's what I thought, but someone—the producers, my co-hosts, maybe the security guards—must have disagreed. After the show, a staff attorney for the network approached me in the hall and said I had to leave the building. I wasn't hiding my concussion symptoms as well as I thought, she said.

"I'm fine," I said. "I can make it through the day."

The attorney insisted I go home, telling me that I needed rest—and that I was also a potential liability.

Graciously, I was escorted out of the building and ushered to a network car. I wasn't taken home, though. I was taken back to the doctor.

There were more tests—pupil dilation, tracking a moving light with my eyes, questions to determine how fast my memory was working. And when we'd run the cognitive gauntlet, the doctor pronounced my concussion worse than he'd originally thought.

"You need to take it easy," he said. "No reading. No television. No screens. Nor work for at least three weeks."

Three weeks?!

It was unfathomable, but the doctor didn't bend to my incredulity. He emphasized how serious it would be if I pushed it, how it might lead to permanent damage, and he told me this might be a good time to be present with my family and friends.

> **Though I should have taken the doctor at his word, though I should have seen it as a sign from God that I needed to slow down and connect with my family, I didn't.**

Though I should have taken the doctor at his word, though I should have seen it as a sign from God that I needed to slow down and connect with my family, I didn't. Instead, I passed the days in mind-numbing boredom. I was antsy. Fidgety. Looking forward to the day I could go back to work. My priorities were out of whack. I'd put all my eggs in the basket of my vocational calling, had forgotten how to be present to God and the people who mattered most to me. And although I'd been given a perfect opportunity to re-center, I didn't. I missed it.

Three weeks passed, and after a Monday afternoon visit to the doctor, I was waiting for the call from the doctor responsible for clearing me from work. A cold snap had fallen across New York, and although John usually walks the mile and change from our home to the train station, I promised I'd drive him to the station. I rolled out of bed that morning at the very last minute, and still in my pajamas—sweatpants and John's T-shirt—made the short jaunt to the train station, John in the passenger side of our family minivan. (It was all much classier than it sounds.) I kissed him at the station, he got out, and I made my way back to the house. While waiting at one of the few stoplights between the station and our house, I received an email from the doctor. I was cleared to go back to work as early as the next day. Just in time for the weekend edition of *GMA*. Elated, I put my phone down and waited for the light to change. When it did, I creeped into the intersection, waiting for an opportunity to turn left. That's when I noticed a car screaming through the red light to my left. It slammed into another car coming through the intersection, and that car veered into my lane, hitting my minivan head-on.

Did my head hit the steering wheel? I don't think so.

Did my seatbelt jerk me back? I'm not sure.

I can't say exactly what happened, but when I got out of the car, the symptoms were back. The headache. The blurry vision. Neck pain. The difficulty processing anything, much less what had just happened. I stumbled out of the car, stunned, and looked at the front of the minivan. It was crushed, totaled. Somehow, I was standing. Somehow, I wasn't bleeding. Still, I knew it—the concussion symptoms were there. I'd just earned another stint out of the office, another season of lying on the couch.

I could have asked God what he might have been trying to say to me. I could have asked whether this adversity was an opportunity to learn something I hadn't. I could have used it as a sort of redo, an opportunity to be present to God, John, and my kids. Still, I didn't. I treated the time just as I had before. It was an annoyance.

Looking back, I can see how jacked up my mindset was. The miscarriage in September hadn't slowed me down (in fact, it had made me push even harder). The apple incident hadn't gotten my attention. The car wreck didn't wake me up either. I was so consumed by what I did that I wasn't able to hear the message God was sending—*Slow down, Paula. Be still.*

By mid-November, I was cleared for the second time. Ready to get back to the hustle, I jumped in with both feet, refusing to slow down. And for a few weeks, things were as they'd always been—*GMA Weekend*, filing reports for the network, hosting the Friday edition of *The View*. I was just as disconnected from my family. Just as out of touch with my faith calling, my purpose. The old Paula was back.

Until she wasn't.

In January, I woke with familiar symptoms. Foggy, throbbing head. Blurred vision. Raging fever. I hadn't been hit in the head with an apple, though, and I hadn't had another car wreck. I hadn't been in a New York City fistfight either, so why did I feel like I'd been beat up?

I made my way to *GMA* that Saturday morning, sat at my desk, and nearly passed out. I was too hot, then too cold. Sweating but still shivering. I pressed through the show that morning, and left the moment we wrapped. I hustled home and took my temperature: *104 degrees—that's not good.* Then I went to my bed and piled nearly every blanket we had on top of me.

When John came home, he was sure I had the flu. So he loaded me into the car and took me to the emergency room. The doctors ran a test, and in no time, confirmed John's suspicion. I had influenza, and because I hadn't taken care of myself while I was coming down with it, I was dehydrated. So the doctors gave me some meds, pumped me full of fluids, and told me to go home and rest.

I returned to work just one week later but hadn't quite recovered. And as I tried to work through the sickness, I found myself unable to control my coughing (more like hacking, really). Weeks into that bout of respiratory trouble, I made my way back to the doctor. They gave me the worst news. What had started as the flu turned to pneumonia.

Really, God?

Since my miscarriage in September of the previous year, my personal life had been one debacle after the next, and in a very real sense, my career had taken a back seat. As I laid on what had become a very familiar couch, I prayed, "What is going on, God?" That's when I heard the still and quiet voice of God.

You have to slow down. You have to find your purpose.

Come again?

Slow down. Find your purpose, Paula. Be still.

In that moment, I knew the truth about my life and what I had to do. I was moving too fast. I had to stop running. I had to be done with *The View*. Done with anchoring the weekend edition of *GMA*. Done with rooting my identity so deeply in my career. It was time to discover why God had called me into this career, this vocation. That meant I had to discover who I was.

Weeks later, I would walk into the Atlantic Grill to have lunch with James Goldston.

The God Who Uses Adversity

If there's one thing I know, it's this: When we get out of whack, when our priorities go askew, God will intervene. He'll give us every opportunity to right our course. Sometimes he'll allow adversity, or even a random apple to get our attention. Sometimes he'll bring the adversity. (Knowing the difference between whether God allows or brings adversity, of course, is tricky business, so it's best to contact your resident theologian when trying to understand your own situation.) And when we're faced with this kind of adversity, we have two possible options: We can run from God, or we can slow down long enough to listen to him and allow him to set a new direction for our lives.

There are plenty of biblical characters who came to hear God through adversity—Jonah, Joseph, and Job, to name just a few. When it comes to God using adversity to wake someone from misdirection of their vocational calling, though, perhaps there is no better example than Saul of Tarsus.

Saul, a Pharisee, was a religious leader of the day, a rising star among first-century Jewish culture. He was from the tribe of Benjamin, was named after a heroic king, and was a Roman citizen. Though he was a young man, he was such an important figure in the religious culture that when the men of Jerusalem stoned Stephen for blasphemy (making him the first Christian martyr), the men stoning Stephen "laid their coats at the feet of a young man named Saul" (Acts 7:58).

Saul was upwardly mobile, climbing the ladder in a hurry. By all accounts, his identity was firmly rooted in his vocational calling. But God wanted to get his attention, wanted to turn this persecutor of Jesus and people into a lover of both.

In the book of Acts, Luke shares Saul's conversion story:

Meanwhile, Saul was still breathing out murderous threats against the Lord's disciples. He went to the high priest and asked him for letters to the synagogues in Damascus, so that if he found any there who belonged to the Way, whether men or women, he might take them as prisoners to Jerusalem. As he neared Damascus on his journey, suddenly a light from heaven flashed around him. He fell to the ground and heard a voice say to him, "Saul, Saul, why do you persecute me?"

"Who are you, Lord?" Saul asked.

"I am Jesus, whom you are persecuting," he replied. "Now get up and go into the city, and you will be told what you must do."

Acts 9:1–6

When Saul got up, he was blind. So he went where God sent him, and waited. (Perhaps he waited on a comfortable couch.)

Days later that same voice came from heaven, this time in a vision of Ananias, a resident of Damascus (and one of the people Saul had set out to persecute). The voice told Ananias to visit the house where Saul was staying, place his hands on his eyes, and restore his sight. Ananias argued at first, saying Saul was an untrustworthy Christian killer. (Um, can you blame him?) God responded: "This man is my chosen instrument to proclaim my name to the Gentiles and their kings and to the people of Israel" (Acts 9:15). So even though it must have felt like adversity to Ananias— marching into the presence of a murderer of his fellow Christians couldn't have been a cakewalk—Ananias obeyed. And after Ananias laid hands on Saul, after he told Saul that he'd been sent so that Saul might see again and be filled with the Holy Spirit, something like scales fell from Saul's eyes. Sight restored, Saul was baptized, and he got to work preaching the Good News of

So many of us have found our identity in the wrong things, and so God still uses a good crisis (or a series of them, in my case) to wake us up from time to time.

Jesus (Acts 9:17–20). Saul, who later became known as Paul, would spend the rest of his life living from a new faith calling—to love God and love people through using whatever gifts he had.

Through adversity, God had gotten Paul's attention. And without wasting any time, he went into the synagogue and began teaching the

Good News of Jesus. It was the start of a lengthy season of ministry, one that included preaching, teaching, and letter-writing campaigns. And as a result of his ministry, we have thirteen of the twenty-seven books of the New Testament.

You might assume things are different today, that God doesn't use such dramatic means to get our attention. But I believe so many of us have found our identity in the wrong things, and so God still uses a good crisis (or a series of them, in my case) to wake us up from time to time. Just ask Jay Williams.

Why Not Me? Basketball Player's Journey through Adversity Manifests Purpose

Jay Williams saunters into the studios of ABC Radio for my podcast interview. He is all smiles as usual, laughing, and before he says a word, I hold up my favorite University of Michigan sweatshirt, which I've carried to the office for just this occasion.

"Really, Paula?" he says before smiling, then hugging me.

Williams was an All-American basketball player for the Duke Blue Devils and no stranger to the Duke-Michigan rivalries of the '90s and early 2000s, so before our interview begins, I want to make my allegiances clear. I'm a Michigan fan first, even if I'm about to interview one of the most celebrated basketball players in Duke history.

Williams's career at Duke couldn't be any more storied. He was a starter for three years, an All-American, the winner of the prestigious Naismith and Wooden Awards, and the college Player of the Year in 2002. He was drafted by the Chicago Bulls with the second overall pick in the 2002 NBA draft. After signing with the team, he was given Michael Jordan's locker. His face was plastered on billboards in Chicago. Analysts projected him to be the most prolific point guard to grace the league. But as bright as his star had been, before he reached the pinnacle of a professional basketball career, he experienced an unexpected vocational shift. It was a shift born in adversity.

We sit across the desk from one another, and Williams fumbles with his microphone as I give him grief about his inability to raise it to the correct speaking level.

"Aren't you supposed to be a professional broadcaster?" I joke.

He laughs, points to the Michigan sweatshirt on the desk, then shoots back. "Hey, is Michigan going to do anything in football this year?"

Touché.

It's the kind of banter I love, between colleagues who've known each other for years. He's been a mainstay over the years at the studio, working first with ESPN—an ABC affiliate—and popping into *GMA* from time to time to report on college basketball or share about his mentoring projects or any number of other things. Familiarity breeds chemistry, but I wonder if Williams doesn't have this kind of chemistry with everyone he meets.

We start rolling, and he shares about his upbringing, how he was raised in a Christian home. His father was Catholic. His mother was Baptist before joining a nondenominational church. He attended a Catholic high school, where he attended mass regularly, recited the Our Father and Hail Mary almost daily, and was surrounded by priests and nuns. Faith was a part of his culture, but it wasn't fully integrated into his life, not until after his accident, he says.

He gives a little context, sharing how he'd graduated early from Duke after three standout years. He'd been drafted by the Chicago Bulls. Expectations were high, and after his first season with the Bulls, he was feeling stronger than ever. He was ready to make a splash in his second year.

On a sunny Chicago day in June 2003, Williams had woken from a post-practice nap and hopped on his motorcycle to make the one-mile jaunt to his agent's house in the Chicago suburbs. They were meeting about Williams's website, and after a productive hour, Williams rose to leave. His agent followed him out the door, where he saw the motorcycle. Williams recalls the conversation with his agent:

As I opened the door, the agent was like, "What are you doing? Why are you riding a bike?" My reasoning to him was, "What do you mean what am I doing? We shouldn't be doing a lot of things. We shouldn't have taken that private plane to Vegas or we shouldn't have been partying with this person or that person."

I interject, reminding him that riding a motorcycle would have nullified his contract with the Bulls. "Yes," he says. "The contract also says you're not allowed to go on Jet Skis; you're not allowed to go skydiving, things you see guys do anyway. . . ."

Williams continues, sharing how he hopped on his bike and pulled from the drive. As he approached the stop sign at the end of the block, he put his bike in neutral, revved the engine once, twice, then a third time. It was the third time that got him.

"In the middle of that third rev, I heard the bike go *click click*. The wheel popped up on me. You know that old saying, *Let go, let God?* I wish I would have done that at that particular time. . . . But I needed to be in control."

He tried to regain composure and muscle the bike back onto the road, he said, but it was no use. The bottom wheel spun out, his trajectory changed, and as he glanced down at the speedometer, he realized he was going nearly 70 miles per hour. That's when he clipped the telephone pole.

"That was the day of my reawakening," he said.

When he came to, his chest was in the grass. His legs, though, were on top of one another, as if he were lying on his side. There was fire in his legs, as if hot water were being poured over them. But when he touched them with his hands, he couldn't feel it. He was going into shock. And just like that, he knew his NBA career was over.

The years following the motorcycle accident would be marked by surgical procedures to repair his severely damaged legs. With the surgeries came confirmation of what he already knew—he was finished playing professional basketball. Years of clinical depression followed, and a cycle of addiction to Oxycontin. He'd had the word *Believe* tattooed on his left wrist years before, and now plagued by suicidal ideation, he tried to cut the word off with a pair of scissors, unconcerned about the possibility of severing an artery.

But as the years passed, something shifted. He began to press more into his faith, more into the spiritual purpose of the accident. He began to see that God could still use him, maybe in more impactful ways. God could use his story to wake up other people.

"It wasn't until a couple of years later that I started to figure out, *Oh wait, this is my purpose.* And the substance of this purpose is so much more meaningful than it would have been if I would have played fifteen years in the NBA," he said. "If I hadn't gone through that pain, how would I have ever understood beauty and purpose?"

> **"The substance of this purpose is so much more meaningful than it would have been if I would have played fifteen years in the NBA."**
> **—Jay Williams**

Williams began to live into his faith for the first time in his life, and as he did, he began to understand the role of adversity in his formation. "Until you really go through some adversity in your life where you have to apply that faith," he said, "you don't have an understanding of it." And as he began to understand it, the anger, the *Why me?* questions passed. "It wasn't until years later," he said, "I recognized the power of saying, 'Wait; why *not* me?'"

He says his whole life had prepared him for that moment, for the gift of a second chance at life. His life had given him shoulders strong enough to carry the new opportunity (his words, not mine). He had an opportunity to overcome adversity by rooting deeper into his faith calling. He had an opportunity to use a new vocation—sports broadcasting—as a conduit to share love with others. And in that realization, things started to change. He began to help others overcome adversity, to learn to live into their own faith callings. As he did, he adopted a simple yet profound lease on life. He sums it up in words that will follow me for months, maybe forever: "When I live, I try to manifest the glory of that purpose."

Adversity Kickstarts Journeys of Faith

To manifest the glory of God's purpose for us—isn't that the call of every person of faith? To live in such a way that the world around us sees our love for God and experiences the love we give to them? Sometimes we lose track of that purpose, this much is true. But when we do, we have every opportunity to correct our course. And sometimes God uses adversity as a way of waking us up, of getting our attention.

Leaving that interview with Williams, I considered how so many of us have moments of awakening, moments when God reaches down in an attempt to get our attention. Those moments can come in so many different ways. They can come through simple things, such as a spouse or child asking for more time. They can come through the birth of a child, or the loss of a family member or friend. They can come through career-ending injuries, or a series of insanely unfortunate events. But when those moments come, it's our job to pay attention to them, to hear the God behind them saying, *Slow down and listen to me; it's time to get reattached to the vine.*

If we mind the messages God is sending, we might find ourselves awakening to the beauty of our true purpose, the beauty of our faith calling. As we do, we'll begin to see the ways God can use our vocational gifts for a higher purpose. That's what happened to Jay Williams. That's what has happened to some of you. That's what happened to me too.

I'd lost track of my true purpose, my true faith calling. But through a series of truly unfortunate events (the Year of Hell, as I've come to call it), God woke me up. And though I didn't know what that might mean for my career—not exactly, anyway—I did the next right thing. I slowed down and reexamined the trajectory of my life. If I kept going in the same direction, I'd lose myself, and maybe my family.

My Year of Hell led me to that conversation with James at the Atlantic Grill, and over the months that followed, I stepped to the side of the spotlight, and I explored what God might have for me. That's how the *Journeys of Faith Podcast with Paula Faris* started. That's how I'd been given the opportunity to interview the likes of David Shedd, Robin Roberts, and Jay Williams. And it was through those interviews that I began to understand the nuances of calling. And if I hadn't taken the time to slow down, to hear the messages God had for me, I might not have had ears to hear the most important lesson, the lesson my dad would teach me: Changed lives, lives of difference, are deeply rooted in the love of God.

CHAPTER 11

The Vine of Faith Calling, the Branches of Vocational Calling

I was on my way home from the city when I received the text that marked the beginning of the end. It was from my mom, and it read,

"HI KIDS, Dad and I are at the ER as he had some dizziness thru the night & was somewhat disoriented at lunch time. The CT scan showed that it looks like he had a mini stroke, so they are keeping him overnight to do an MRI. HE FEELS OKAY NOW BUT THEY WANT TO DO FURTHER TESTING. Please pray all goes well. Love you!"

I tried calling my mom, but she didn't answer. Maybe she was on the phone with my sister or talking with a doctor, but whatever the case, the text was only mildly alarming. A ministroke—folks recover from those all the time, right? Maybe Dad needed to change his diet a little, eat more cold-water fish and less red meat. Exercise more. That sort of thing. And though a stay in the hospital is never good, maybe this would be a sort of wake-up call.

As soon as I stepped off the set, before even making my way back to my dressing room, I called my mom and told her I was coming home.

Later in the evening, I got in touch with my mom, and she said Dad seemed to be okay. She attached a photo; he was hooked up to all kinds of machines, but he was flashing his signature smile and had a twinkle in his eye. The doctors would figure it out, she said, and I shouldn't worry. So I said another prayer, gave John the update, and then turned back to my notes for the following day.

It was a busy week. I was filling in for Robin on *GMA* all week, and the next morning as I made my way to the set, I kept my phone close. Sure enough, just after the first hour of the show, and while in a commercial break, I received a text from my sister.

> Hi Sibs-
> Mom asked me to update all of you. She got a call from the nurse this morning. Dad has declined since last night. His speech is slurred and some weakness in his right side. They have been treating him for stroke, but he still has not had a conclusive MRI. Mom was getting ready to head out the door when she called me. Let's step up the prayers.

It was news I wasn't expecting, and it caught me off guard. As I reread the message, my head started spinning, my ears ringing. I didn't realize I was crying until a tear hit my phone screen. Was this real? How were his symptoms worsening?

I told George and Michael—my co-anchors for the morning—I was going to need a little time backstage through the next commercial break, and they agreed, seeing that something was going on. After that break, I gained my composure as best I could, touched up my makeup, took a few deep breaths, and finished the last hour of the show. As soon as I stepped off the set, before even making my way back to my dressing room, I called my mom and told her I was coming home. She asked me to wait a day because there were more tests to run and she was overwhelmed. I didn't like it, but I agreed. I bought plane tickets for Caroline and me, and after Thursday's edition of *GMA*, we made our way to Michigan.

The next afternoon, Caroline and I walked into my dad's room. A feeding tube ran through his nose, cords attached all over his body, electrical diodes dotting his chest. The covers were barely on him. I wasn't ready for this.

"Hey, Dad."

He looked at me with a helpless smile as I leaned in for a kiss.

It was a one-sided conversation for the most part, Caroline and I swapping stories while he responded by raising his eyebrows, occasionally pushing out a chuckle. On a couple of occasions, he tried to talk, but to his great frustration, he couldn't.

Mom and a family friend, Jon Throne, entered the room. Mom said that when Dad was released, there would be months of rehab. He'd have to relearn to use his right side. They needed to make decisions about rehab. There was an option in nearby Chelsea, Mom said, but if that didn't work out, we'd have to choose between a facility in Lansing (the home of the Michigan State Spartans) and one in Ann Arbor (the University of Michigan Wolverine den). I raised my voice, said there was *no way* they were taking my dad to Spartan country; we were Wolverines. I went on and on, and when I finished my faux rant, I looked at my dad with a wink and a nod, and he gathered enough strength to let out a full-bore belly laugh. It was so big, in fact, I wondered whether I might have induced another stroke, and I asked my dad to take it easy. He obliged, a tear trickling from the corner of his right eye.

The doctor entered, told us Dad was suffering repeated strokes, and the medical team was stumped. They'd sort it out, he said, and although Dad should regain the ability to swallow, speak, eat, and drink, he might not fully regain the use of his right side. There were still tests to run—an arterial CT scan to determine whether there were any blood clots in the veins of his throat and neck, more blood work, some strength tests. That's when I made out my dad's first real words, which seemed to carry heat and come out of nowhere.

"I want to get out of here."

"It'll be a few more days," the doctor said.

My dad rose a raspy objection. "A few more days?!"

(The doctors would later tell me that anger and frustration tap into a different part of the brain, which is why he was easier to understand when he was angry or frustrated.)

The doctor apologized, and he and Mom walked into the hall. Dad did his best to put on a brave face, looking at me, smiling. I sat next to his bed, and moments later, tears streamed down his cheeks. I turned to closed-ended, yes-or-no questions, trying not to make him speak too much.

"Are you peaceful, Dad?" He nodded in agreement.

"Would you rather go to heaven than live like this?" Again, he nodded.

From August of 2018 to February of 2019, my dad made the slow march to eternity. He never regained his ability to eat, drink, swallow, or speak. His right side remained paralyzed. His muscles cramped, causing him so much pain. There were times you could understand what he was trying to say, but for the most part, it was indecipherable. He laughed a little, smiled as much as he could, but even that was becoming a chore. My dad was wasting away, and there wasn't anything we could do about it.

Over those months, Dad received all his calories and all his water through a feeding tube. We watched helplessly as he shed weight. I flew home every few weeks, and when I wasn't there, I'd call Mom to see whether there'd been any improvement, holding my breath as I hoped to hear Dad was making a miraculous comeback. Time after time, my mom gave similar reports.

Your dad lost another five pounds.

He's down twenty pounds.

He's lost forty pounds.

I don't know how much weight he can lose.

He's crying a lot and doesn't seem to know what's going on.

His body and mind—I think they're wasting away, Paula.

In November, three months after the stroke, I flew home, determined to take him to one final Michigan football game. I wanted to experience the Big House (the nickname for the University of Michigan football stadium) one last time with him, so we loaded him into a transport van and made the trek to Ann Arbor. We sat in the stadium that Saturday afternoon, and I held his hand as we cheered for the Wolverines. When Michigan scored, he half-smiled. I leaned down, asked him if he knew where we were, and in an exhausted, exasperated intonation, he all but shouted, "Yes!"

My dad, who would have been singing the Michigan fight song at the top of his lungs the year before, was barely responsive, and when he was, he seemed uncomfortable. It wasn't how I imagined our last football outing, but still, we were together. And that meant everything to me. Still does.

November gave way to December, December to a new year. And by February 2019, Dad was ready to go home. My mom consulted us kids and finally made the gut-wrenching decision to remove the feeding tube on February 5. I was working the day they removed the feeding tube, on a publicity tour in Nashville, Tennessee, for my new podcast. And when I got back to my hotel, I walked to my suitcase, pulled out my dad's U.S. Marine Corps hat, put it on, and fell into my bed, crying myself to sleep.

Days later, the whole family descended on Jackson, knowing that without food, any breath could be his last. For a few days, we took turns holding his hand and sponging his lips to keep his mouth from drying out. We told him we loved him, and we sang his favorite songs. We anointed him with oil, prayed over him. We watched as he slipped in and out of consciousness. We surrounded him with love and shared stories.

When Dad was lucid, he cried a good bit, but on the Saturday before he died, he cried more than usual. I asked why he was crying.

"Daddy, are you crying because you're in pain?"

He shook his head. No.

"Daddy, are you crying because you're sad?"

He shook his head again. No.

"Daddy, are you crying because you're overwhelmed by the love and memories?"

Yes, he nodded. And I knew he meant it. He was living his life, full of joy.

When I wasn't by my dad's bedside, I rummaged through his things (with Mom's permission, of course). In the office room, shoved in a corner, I found an unassuming box filled with loose papers and journals. Had it been opened in years? Did Mom know about these boxes? Had he left it behind for me to discover? (I was certain he had, though I won't know until I see my dad on the other side.)

I pulled out the tattered papers, started reading, and realized these tattered papers were pieces of a falling-apart journal. As I read, it was as if I'd entered a time machine. I read about his struggles with anxiety, his worry; I followed his journey. In his journals, he wrote of his early home life, of the ways his Lebanese father criticized him, put him down, and dismissed him. He wrote of how he'd run away from home, how he'd chased booze, women, career advancement. In one entry, he wrote of his early days of fast living, "My night began at 11:30 p.m. and I went from bar to bar. I tried to have a life with God, but it was too empty."

In another entry, he wrote of his career, "I was out for a better job, higher pay, a very independent life. Trying to make it on my own, I was critical of others and craved material possessions." He wrote of his problems with authority, how his temper often swelled out of control. He was anxious on the job, which led to anxiety at home, which led to a deep depression, which led to marital problems.

Mom didn't understand him in those early years, he wrote, and he wondered whether she did things just "*to get under my skin.*" (Yes, he underlined it for emphasis.) He didn't know how to react, except to get angry and blow up, which wasn't helping things either. He was ready to "pack her bags and send her back home" to live with her parents in St. Louis. So patriarchal. Such a 1950s mentality. I chuckled.

And if marriage pushed most of his buttons, parenting pushed all of them. Because he hadn't connected with his own father, he wasn't exactly sure how to connect with us. He did his best, of course. Still, he wrote,

> I could not stand to watch their mistakes and did not have any pa-
> tience with them. When they accidentally spilled the milk or broke
> something, I would raise my voice at them, and they would shudder
> at me. I really wanted children but did not know how to cope with
> them. My discipline was totally unloving. At times, I would really
> let them have it for having done something I didn't like.

I knew my sisters had experienced this side of my dad, but the truth was, I hadn't. Then again, by the time I started making memories, Dad was already a changed man. Mostly because he'd met a community that loved God and loved him, and they had taught him to do the same.

I followed my dad's progression as he wrote about becoming more and more involved in Morning Star Christian Community. That community of faith loved him and my mother, taught them how to live into true faith. They were a community that showed compassion through my parents' struggles and helped them understand how to listen better, be more patient, and love each other more completely. As Mom and Dad grew in the community, they grew closer to God, closer together, and they both grew in their approach to parenting. As my dad grew in his faith, he also grew in his perspective on raising children. We'd become the joy of his life instead of a constant frustration. We were people to be loved rather than mastered. And because of his great love for us, he passed up opportunities for advancement so he could have more time with us. He made sure he was home by dinner each night. He spent time with us on the weekends instead of going into the office.

I read and read for hours, following my dad's journey from journal to journal, reading along

> My dad had rooted into his faith calling and allowed it to change the orientation of his life. He expressed his faith calling in every facet of his life, and when death came calling, he was ready.

in his distinctive, engineer-meticulous handwriting. His heart lined along the pages, I began to see him in a different light. The man I'd always known as so strong, so supportive, so courageous, had endured his own seasons of struggle. His twenties and thirties were just as angsty as anyone else's, but somehow he'd managed to find the secret to living the good life. He'd rooted into his faith calling—to love God and love people—and he'd allowed it to change the orientation of his life. It changed the way he interacted with my mom, with us, with his coworkers, and with the Morning Star community. It affected the jobs he accepted and the ones he didn't. He expressed his faith calling in every facet of his life, and as a result, when death came calling, he was ready.

With the feeding tube out, it was only a matter of time. But being the U.S. Marine my dad was, he hung on for ELEVEN DAYS without food and virtually no water. And in the days before he passed, my sisters and I stayed by his bedside at the hospice facility. But on Valentine's

Day, my mom asked us to give them a little space, and we obliged. We were on our way back to the facility the following day when we got the call. Dad had received a visit from his pastor and the hospice chaplain that morning. After the hospice chaplain left, he was alone for ten minutes. That's when he chose to take his final breath.

At the funeral, my Caroline sang the words "Well done, my good and faithful one" over my dad (a line from the song "Well Done" by The Afters), and if anyone's ever heard those words in eternity, I'm sure it was him. He was the best man I've ever known, and if you could have seen the crowd that showed up for his funeral, if you could have listened to the ways they remembered him, you might be convinced too. And it was all because he'd been firmly rooted in his faith calling. He knew who he was and what he'd been called to be—a representation of God's love to the world.

In the days after his death, the days in which I wrote this book, I considered my dad's life and settled into the most important question: How did I want to be remembered? When I passed, did I want John, my kids, and my friends to remember I was preoccupied with my vocational calling, with the jobs I did? Or did I want them to remember who I was—*Paula Faris, the beloved of God, who lived so in touch with that love that she shared it with the world.*

I'd already stepped away from *The View* and the weekend edition of *GMA*. I'd already begun carving out my niche as a faith podcaster for ABC News. But I still hadn't put all the pieces together. I didn't fully appreciate how rooting our identity in our faith calling, making all our decisions from that rooting, changes everything. The truth was, my vocational calling could change from time to time, as long as the decision to make the change grew from my faith calling. I could move to another show, another location, another media avenue (such as a podcast). I could branch out, as long as I remained connected to the vine, rooted into my faith calling. As long as I was using my vocation as a vehicle for that love, I was living from the center of my purpose.

The Vine, the Branches

Before my dad found God, he bounced around from job to job, always looking for the next better gig. He thought his restlessness could be cured by more money, more success, more opportunity. But all that changed after he defined himself by *who he was* instead of *what he did*. After he met God, he settled into his job as an engineer at Sparton Corporation in Jackson, Michigan, and he never left. Never sought advancement either. Instead, he made intentional vocational choices, refusing to climb the ladder of corporate success. When all his peers were gunning for the next promotion, the next raise, the next advancement, he kept his head down, worked hard, and did his best to shine his light in the world around him. He turned down promotions, mostly because those promotions would cut into his family time.

In a sense, my dad chose a career path quite different from his peers. He opted to stay smaller for the sake of his family, and he did it all because he wanted to spend more time with God, mom, us, and his community. He wanted to live a life rooted in purpose instead of one rooted in promotion.

My dad demonstrated how living a life of purpose requires firm rooting in your faith calling. It requires knowing why you're doing what you're doing and who you are doing it for. It means never deviating from the *why* no matter what path you choose. But how do you stay rooted in your faith calling when the world puts so much pressure on you to work the next hour, make the next dollar, go after the next big promotion? By remaining attached to who you are in God, by rooting into your faith calling. Just like my dad did.

Jesus tells us in John 15:1, 4, "I am the true vine, and my Father is the gardener. . . . No branch can bear fruit by itself; it must remain in the vine." This verse is not primarily about vocational calling. It applies to all of life. If we're to bear fruit in the Christian life—whether at home, in our communities, or in our vocations—we have to remain fixed to Jesus, rooted in him. We have to be about the things he was about and moving in the ways he wants us to move. We have to draw all our wisdom, all our strength, all our sustenance from the true vine. We have to let God direct all our outcomes.

When it comes to our vocational calling, rooting into the vine might mean doing what my dad did: passing up career opportunities and slowing down so that he could be more present to his family, friends, and community. It might mean acting on other opportunities, though. It could mean taking the promotion, or changing career fields, or becoming a freelancer, or stepping away from your career to be a stay-at-home wife or husband so that you can express the love of God to various people in different ways. No matter the branch of your vocational calling, though, if it's not rooted in the true vine of faith calling, if it's not supported and nourished by God's life, it won't bear fruit. And what does Jesus say about branches not rooted in the vine, branches not bearing fruit?

> He cuts off every branch in me that bears no fruit, while every branch that does bear fruit he prunes, so that it will be even more fruitful.
>
> John 15:2

Looking at my own career, I suppose I could say it had been fruitful in a certain sense. There were times I expressed my faith calling, my purpose through my career. I'd been open about my faith, had shared God's love with people. But was my vocational calling completely rooted in my faith calling? *Hardly.* So God pruned away (using the Year of Hell, no less), ultimately calling me to take a step back and reevaluate my vocational options. As I did, as God revealed the ways I'd rooted my identity in the wrong things—my own career—he helped me correct my course. He helped me find new identity in him. He helped me see how I could use my vocational skills to spread a different message—a message of faith and purpose.

The Changing Branches of Vocational Calling (Your Vocation Can Change!)

God doesn't prune our vocational branches only because we've misplaced our identity. Sometimes he prunes them even when we're healthy so that we might share his love in different ways with different people. Consider John, the love of my life. He loved being a basketball coach, and he gave so much to it. He was successful, and not just because he had a great basketball mind and good work ethic. He was successful because he was a gifted leader. But the transient nature of my career required John to give up coaching. It was a sort of pruning, one John was able to endure because he hadn't rooted his identity in what he did. He knew who he was, and he lived from the deep core of his belief that God would lead him to where he was supposed to be.

So when God called him to use his natural leadership skills in commercial real estate, he was ready. Because of that transition, he now manages 150 people in the NYC branch of Marcus & Millichap, one of the city's largest commercial real estate firms. Attached to the vine, willing to have branches pruned, he'd been given even greater opportunity. While John's vocational gifting (leadership and strategic thinking) hadn't changed, his vocational calling had.

> **God doesn't prune our vocational branches only because we've misplaced our identity. Sometimes he prunes them even when we're healthy.**

I also consider my friend (and the person who helped me bring this book to life) Seth Haines. Graduating from law school, scoring at the top of his state's bar exam, he accepted a position at a prestigious law firm. He climbed the ranks, was named partner, and for twelve years he did the lawyer gig. But after a season of stress related to the medical condition of his youngest son, a season of heavy drinking to cope with the struggle, he woke to the fact that he wasn't living from his true faith calling to love God and love others. He sobered up, experienced the love of God, and wrote about it in a book entitled *Coming Clean*, hoping he could share the love he experienced with those struggling with addiction ("any old addiction," as he puts it). As a result of that book, he resigned his partnership, became a writer and editor, and now he helps people like me steward the message God has given them (all while maintaining a legal practice). Knowing who he is and what his purpose is, he uses his vocational gifts (writing, collaboration, and creativity) to bring the love of God to the page, all for the sake of others. Again, his unique vocational gifts didn't change, but his specific vocational calling did.

It's not just people in the early or middle stages of their careers who experience vocational pruning so they can bear more fruit. Consider my mom, for instance. The day of the funeral came and went. My dad's body was laid in the grave. I decided to spend one more day with Mom before I headed back to New York. She sat at the kitchen table after breakfast, wearing something approximating panic.

"I don't know what I'll do without your dad around," she said. "For fifty-three years I've had the same job: to be a mother and a wife."

I held her hand, and because of my own journey, because I'd been thinking and writing about calling, I considered the words of David Shedd. What was Mom curious about? What were her innate giftings? What could I encourage her in? Hadn't she always been curious about singing, dancing, and acting? Didn't she always float about the house singing a tune, and hadn't she often mentioned being in a local theater production?

I reminded my mom of her natural gifts and talents, and she smiled. She'd always been too busy tending to us, or Dad, or the community at Morning Star, she said. But now we were all out of the house, Dad was in eternity, and she still had tons of energy and enthusiasm.

"You should consider trying out for a play in the local theater," I suggested.

The beginnings of a smile crept across her face. Her eyes were a little brighter. Maybe she should, she said.

There's no telling whether my mom will go through with it, whether she'll actually try out for a production at Center Stage, Jackson's community theater, but the fact remains: Just because she's in the later years of her life doesn't mean she hasn't been given a new vocational calling, some way to express the love of God to the world around her. She has a new opportunity, and knowing her as I do, I know she'll find a way to share her purpose, her faith calling, with others through some new vocational avenue, even at eighty years of age.

Vocational Pruning Is a Lifelong Experience

Rooting into your faith calling, living from who you are might require you to sacrifice career advancement, as it did my dad. It might require you take a step back from your upward trajectory too, as in my case. Rooting into your faith calling might require you to apply your innate vocational skills to another industry altogether as John did, or use your skills across industries as Seth does. And when one season of your life gives way to the next, you may have to find a new vocation through which to express your faith calling, as my mom is doing. No matter the situation, no matter the season, one thing is certain: A life of purpose is one that is attached to the root of our faith callings, one that is nourished by it, one that bears fruit in our day-to-day vocations.

Because I like the tree analogy (roots, vines, and branches), I'll go out on a limb and guess that most of us would rather be known for who we are than for what we do. We'd rather be known as people who lived in the love of God. We would hope the people who come to our funerals would say, "She was a great friend and was always present," or "She really loved her husband well," or "His kids are better because of his life." As for me, I hope people say more than, "She was a really good reporter."

Living the kind of life you want to be remembered by, the kind of life my dad lived, doesn't happen without rooting. It doesn't happen without knowing who you are in God and who he's made you to be. It doesn't happen without being clear in your faith calling.

If I've known anyone who lived life well, it was my dad. He was a flawed man, sure. He had his parental shortcomings, and I'm not sure he ever beat his insecurities. But he ultimately found purpose in who he was, not in what he did. He loved God. He loved his family. End of story. His journals proved as much. And his epitaph makes no mention of what he did. His epitaph describes who he was —*Loving Husband, Father, and Gido.* I had a front-row seat to that kind of life, and though I hadn't paid attention for so long, in February of 2019 I decided not to take my dad's example for granted anymore. I decided to do my best, flawed as I am, to live the same kind of life. And I decided to invite my children into the process.

CHAPTER 12

The Journey to Faith through Incremental Change

I walk into the building at 47 West 66th Street starving and need-ing coffee. Thirty minutes before, I'd ordered coffee at the Starbucks across the street from the train station near my home in Westchester County, New York (I didn't take a car into the city that morning be-cause I wasn't doing *GMA*), but the line was long, the baristas were swamped, and I was late. So after five minutes waiting for my decaf coffee with a shot of peppermint, cream on the side, I bolted without picking up my drink. I couldn't be late for the interview. If I was, Dan Harris would give me grief for all of eternity.

I make my way to the ABC cafeteria, looking for a cup of coffee and a snack. As I do, I consider the course of my career since that conversation with James in the Atlantic Grill almost a year ago. When I left that lunch with James, I was at a vocational crossroads. I couldn't have said it at the time, but I needed to root more into my faith calling, needed to come to a better understanding of who God created me to be and how to share his love with the world. And knowing I needed to learn how to integrate faith and vocation, I figured many others might too. Could there be a better way to learn together than through a faith podcast?

It seems unfathomable. James had been so accommodating, so open to new possibilities. He'd caught the vision for the podcast even before I was completely sure about it, and he gave me plenty of latitude to pull it together. Even more, he gave me the space I needed away from my day-to-day on-air duties, which allowed me the time to brainstorm the podcast. That wasn't all, though. The space helped me reconnect with John. It allowed me to spend more time with the kids too, and more days than not, I'm there when they get home from school. Availability, balance, reconnection—it's been so good. And if it were just about the reconnection, that would be enough. But the work has been so much more meaningful than I ever could have imagined.

I pour coffee into a paper cup, grab a vegan protein bar (Dan, the agnostic Buddhist vegan, loves stuff like this), pay, and head for the ABC Radio studios on the second floor, where we record most of the podcasts. Work has been so rewarding over this last year, and I remember the interviews, the moments that have marked *Journeys of Faith*.

David Shedd taught me how each of us has an underlying purpose, which is fueled by our faith calling, our purpose. He showed me how that faith calling should always be the fuel of our vocational callings, and how we can identify those vocational callings (what are we good at, what are we curious about, and what are the skills and proficiencies our mentors and trusted advisors recognize?).

Robin Roberts taught me I couldn't let fear paralyze me and keep me from pursuing the work God had prepared for me, that I had to cultivate a desire that was bigger than that fear and step out of my comfort zone.

Michael Strahan helped me understand how fear attacks us all, how it sometimes manifests in impostor syndrome, especially as we move from one branch of our vocation to the next.

Bishop Jakes taught me that the only way to push through the fear of impostor syndrome is to let what I do flow from who I am in God.

Jay Williams taught me that when we lose our way, when we put too much of our identity in what we do, God will allow adversity to get us back on track, to help us root our identities in our faith calling.

Overcoming fear and insecurity and rooting deep into our faith calling is possible, particularly when surrounded by a loving, faith-oriented community.

And my dad—through his death, the journals he left, and the life he lived—showed me that overcoming fear and insecurity and rooting deep into our faith calling is possible, particularly when surrounded by a loving, faith-oriented community.

Through producing the podcast, I've discovered that calling can't be reduced to simple notions of vocation or occupation, even though our churches, synagogues, mosques, and temples might tell us differently. Calling is so much bigger than that, and it begins in who we are in God and what we were ultimately put on this earth for—to be a representation of God's love, his hands and feet in this world. I've learned that our vocational calling, what we do, is nothing more than the vehicle by which we express that faith calling, the way we're uniquely equipped to love God and love people in the world. And in this understanding, I've noticed something else: how I'd gotten it all *so wrong*.

It took a meltdown in my personal life to wake me up. Knowing what I know now, I can see how my Year of Hell was God's way of slowing me down, of changing my priorities. And when I slowed down, when I made the change I felt he was calling me into, I was able to see. When I was afraid I wasn't good enough, lacking self-esteem and self-worth, I'd almost not pursued God's leading into journalism. And once I was a journalist, the fear of failure and the fear that I wasn't good enough or capable enough led me by the nose. Fear of failure drove me to overwork. Fear that I wasn't capable enough drove me to overachieve. It led me to search for identity and meaning through success in my vocational calling. But the Year of Hell, the slowdown, it led me to ask the right questions, talk to the right people, and find the right answer.

I walk into the studio, set my coffee down, and open my vegan protein bar, which has peanuts and chocolate in it, so how bad could it be? One bite is all it takes. I'm done. Finished. Wanting bacon now. How can anyone eat like this? I remind myself to ask Dan.

I sit in my chair, waiting for my dear friend, and although I'd usually take time to review my notes, I don't need to for this interview. My questions for Dan are all in my head and my heart.

I daydream, grateful for the success of the new podcast. We'd hit the top of the faith charts on iTunes not long after launching. Wouldn't that have been exactly what wound my clock in years past? Yeah. And true enough, it still felt good, but rankings and numbers didn't really motivate me anymore. There'd been a subtle, slow shift over the last year. Now I was motivated by something else. I guess walking away from two dream jobs—*The View* and *GMA Weekend*—reoriented me. I guess it helped me discover the true purpose of my career, my vocation, to use my unique gifts and talents to love God and love people.

Dan walks into the office, smiling. He's dressed down today, not in his usual pressed suit and starched shirt. (Dan is the kind of guy who wears a dress shirt to his kid's school carnival, and he'd readily admit that.) It's a familial look, casual, and I tell him it looks good on him. We hug, and he asks whether it'll be odd to have an agnostic Buddhist on the show. I shake my head. After all, isn't every way of thinking about God—about his existence or even the lack thereof—an act of faith? Besides, I say, I've been the little sister he never had nor wanted (one of our many jokes), and I know our listeners will want the dirt on the many faith conversations we've had off camera over the years. We take our seats and start rolling.

Sitting at the desk across from me, Dan shares his own faith background. He was a Boston boy, raised by a nominally Jewish father and a scientist mother who was "more of an atheist than anything." He never attended worship services, and there was no presence of organized religion in his family, at least not until he was in the seventh grade. As many of his Jewish classmates approached their thirteenth birthdays, Dan shares, they began attending Hebrew school in preparation for their bar mitzvahs. Loving a good party and the cash presents that came with any bar mitzvah, Dan wanted in on the action, so he convinced his mom and dad to enroll him in a progressive Hebrew school so he could prepare for his own celebration. After he completed his stint in Hebrew school, his parents threw him a bar mitzvah (which netted him a few thousand dollars, he mentions). But that was it for his religious exploration, he says. The deeper practices of faith never stuck. Transcendent questions weren't piqued. He never looked for some deeper, cosmic meaning. Just as his mother had once told him, he considered God and Santa Claus on equal footing—both myths.

Dan wouldn't come back to questions of faith until his early days in journalism, he says. In 2000 he made his way to ABC News, and as soon as he arrived, iconic anchorman Peter Jennings took him under his wing. Jennings wasn't particularly religious (though he might have been raised Christian, Dan mentions), but he was a visionary and he understood that Americans deeply cared about faith. So early in Dan's career, Jennings approached him with an assignment.

"You, Dan, are going to cover faith and spirituality," Dan recalls Jennings saying. Dan's response?

"I do not want to do that; I'm not interested in it at all."

Jennings's reply?

"He didn't care. He said, 'You're going to do it.'"

And that was that.

It was that assignment that led Dan into the world of faith and spirituality, and he began rubbing shoulders with the movers and shakers of the faith world. Megachurch pastors. Jewish rabbis. Spiritualists like Eckhart Tolle. It was an eye-opening experience, if not enlightening. "As I covered religion," he says, "I saw I was truly ignorant about the issues." So he started making friends with the subjects of the religious stories he covered and, as he put it, those friends exposed his prejudices against faith. He began to see how huge swaths of people were looking for meaning in the cosmos. They'd discovered that meaning through connection with God, and that, he said, wasn't a terrible thing. So though being a religious correspondent didn't inspire him to accept or reject faith one way or the other, it didn't drive him deeper into his antagonisms either. In fact, there were some people of faith who were intriguing to him, some whom he respected deeply.

"Gabe Lyons is . . . a friend of mine, who I find very interesting," he says. I know Gabe and Rebekah Lyons very well (both are leaders in the Christian world), but only because Dan introduced us. "Gabe has described a practice . . . I think he calls it something like 'Jesus goggles,' where he's sort of walking around the streets wearing goggles [obviously imaginary ones] through which he views everyone as Jesus might."

"It's his lens," I interject.

"Yes," he says. Then pointing to his own heart and leaning in, he asks, "Can I view everyone with that kind of compassion and friendliness? That is very close to the Buddhist practice of developing a friendly attitude toward yourself and others. To me that is very intriguing. I think the best faith operates in that realm."

There it is, the echo of purpose, of faith calling. He wouldn't say his foundational calling is to love God, but still we share common ground—take the love we receive and share it with others. Extend compassion, generosity, and friendliness. And even though we disagree on the particulars of the source of that compassion, generosity, and love, I know Dan isn't just blowing smoke about his own desire to cultivate this kind of compassion. I've seen a significant change in his life since he began pursuing that kind of compassionate life through the use of mindful meditation. And as we continue to talk about the importance of developing a compassionate worldview, Dan shares the way forward.

> When we leave this world, what will be remembered is the way we loved God and loved others. Our vocations and careers are simply the mechanism, the conduit, for doing that.

"I have a lot of work to do, but I'm mister 10 percent." By that, he means that if he can increase his happiness, his compassion, his understanding toward others by 10 percent, he's on the right track. "I don't believe there are silver bullets," he says. "I think change happens incrementally over time."

There it is, the wisdom I've become so accustomed to hearing from Dan. It's not a complicated truth, but even as he says it, it settles into me. I didn't overcome all my fears overnight, and sometimes my fear of failure still crops up. I didn't learn to root into my faith calling in one singular moment either, and there are days I still find too much of my identity in my work. But little by little, I'm understanding how faith informs my vocational calling, how it asks me to do things that are bigger than my fear, and how when I root my identity in that faith, God makes the path forward plain. Incrementally, I'm learning the secret that my dad understood so well— when we leave this world, what will be remembered is the way we loved God and loved others. Our vocations and careers are simply the mechanism, the conduit, for doing that. Everything else, every other success, promotion, raise, or opportunity, is just extra, the cherry on top.

Dan and I wind our way through the rest of the podcast, talking of life and death, and notions of eternity. We talk about my certainty of the afterlife and his uncertainty of it. I tell him of my certainty that I'll see my dad again, and he doesn't dismiss me, doesn't make fun of me. In fact, he says it's beautiful.

We talk for almost an hour, and when we've nearly exhausted the topic of faith and God, I wind down the interview.

"Love you, Friend."

These were my last words to Dan before we wrapped. And I meant them.

Teaching Our Kids to Ask the Right Questions

Wisdom can come from all places and all people. Sometimes it comes from a sermon or a trusted Christian friend. (Someone like Gabe or Rebekah Lyons, for instance.) Often it comes from the pages of Scripture. But sometimes I stumble upon it, almost as if by accident. Dan, my agnostic Buddhist friend who first encouraged me in my efforts to start a faith podcast and write this book, shared the wisdom of incremental change with me. In my dad's death, I stumbled upon the gift of perspective. I see how incremental change led him to love my mom, us kids, and his community better. And that's the kind of life I want. It's the kind of life I want for my kids.

While visiting my sister in South Carolina after Dad passed, I was reading a book to Landon, my preschooler. It wasn't a particularly compelling book, not one with some grandiose moral or teachable point. There was a dump truck involved. And as I read it, I was bored out of my mind. (I'm mildly ashamed to admit it, but I'm not the kind of mom who loves reading with, or to, her kids.) As he sat on my lap, I stopped reading and asked the question that popped into my head, almost without thinking.

"Landon, what do you want to do when you grow up?"

No sooner had the words come out of my mouth than I pulled myself up short. Though I'd learned so much about vocation in the months since my conversation with James, I'd fallen into the typical societal trap. I was inadvertently teaching Landon his worth was in *what he did* instead of the kind of *person he was*. And in that moment, one singular thought came screaming into my brain.

Oh my gosh, society sucks and so do I!

Before Landon could answer the wrong question, I said, "You know what, buddy, forget that. Let's go get some juice."

As we walked to the fridge, I wondered how I might engage with him in a different kind of conversation, one that revolved around the right questions and invited him to root into who he is and what kind of person he is and wants to be. Being versus doing—we could start there. So I offered a simple statement, one I hoped he'd remember.

"You know what buddy? What you do doesn't matter as much as the kind of person you are. You know?"

He looked up at me, smiled, and said, "Yup!" I wasn't sure the message stuck, but it was a starting place, a building block. I poured a glass of juice for Landon and considered how many opportunities I'd blown, opportunities to direct my kids into their faith calling, into what kind of person they'd want to be rather than what they wanted to do for a living.

I remembered when Caroline came to me the summer after her fifth-grade year. Only ten years old and she'd had an idea. She wanted to join some kind of bike across America campaign after she completed the sixth grade. I pushed, asking her what the campaign was all about, but she couldn't quite say. I pressed harder, asked why she'd want to do something if she didn't really know the cause behind the campaign. Her answer was astounding: "It'll look good on my college applications."

I nearly fainted. Sure, Caroline had always been an overachiever, but to be thinking about college applications at just ten years old? Come on. And yet, could I blame her? She'd only been doing what society (and so many of us parents) had trained her to do: run after achievement and vocational success.

Considering my moment with Landon, pondering Caroline's question, I came to a simple conclusion: Something is fundamentally broken with our society when we care so much about success that we slam preschoolers with questions of vocation and when fifth-graders are considering résumé-builders for college admissions. But it wasn't just Caroline. That very month, news had broken about a college admissions scandal, one in which wealthy parents who cared so much about what their children would do that they were willing to compromise who they were. Weeks before, I'd watched that news unfold. Rich and famous parents had allegedly paid thousands of dollars to a college admission "consultant" to inflate ACT and SAT scores, and to create fake athletic records. Why? It was a scheme designed to secure admission to schools like the University of Southern California, Stanford, the University of Texas, Georgetown, and Yale. And if it was true, didn't this confirm that our society, our system, was rooted in the wrong thing? Didn't it confirm that we'll do anything to achieve in *what we do*, even if it means perpetrating criminal fraud?

Later that evening, John and I sat in pool chairs, talking. I shared the moment with Landon and recalled my conversation with Caroline. I told John I wanted something different for our kids. I wanted to start them down the road of faith calling, a road on which they could grow deeply rooted in who they were—children loved by God—so that they would share the love of God with the world around them. I wanted them to realize that the vocational gifts they've been given are simply the unique way they are called to go about loving God and loving people.

John nodded in agreement, and said we could still cultivate Caroline's inclination toward the arts, toward singing, dancing, and performing. We could still give JJ the tools he needs to be successful in sports, natural athlete that he is. I added that we could cultivate whatever Landon's unique skills turned out to be, though his most promising skills to date are telling fart jokes and navigating fart apps. (I know I'm not helping him grow out of it either, because I always laugh.) After all, there's nothing wrong with giving our kids the tools for success or teaching them that excellence matters. But it only matters as far as it gives them the ability to use their vocational calling to share their faith calling.

It was a moment of marital agreement. Instead of teaching our kids to pursue success at all costs, we would teach them to live a different way. We would start asking them, "Who do you want to be when you grow up?" instead of, "What do you want to do when you grow up?" We would teach them their gifts are the way in which God will ask them to share his love with the world. We would teach them to build faithful lives, lives like my dad's. Maybe this could be the legacy he left behind.

The Journey of Faith—An Invitation to Incremental Change

Perhaps you can locate yourself in my story. Maybe you see yourself in the beginning, knowing you've been called to do something different with your life. Maybe you know God is calling you to use your unique gifts to spread his love through a different vocational calling, but you're too scared to make the leap of faith, too scared to branch out. Maybe you're in the right vocation but you're plagued by fear of failure, by the fear that you don't belong, so you compensate by overworking or trying to overachieve. Maybe you've rooted your entire identity in your vocation, even to the exclusion of the things you care about most, such as your spouse, your kids, and your community of faith. If that's you, here's the good news: You don't have to change everything overnight (nor do you have to wait for a year of hell to wake you up). You can begin to correct your course today by making a simple paradigm shift and seeking incremental change.

The paradigm shift? See your vocation for what it is. It's what you do, and it doesn't define you. Understand your vocation is meant to be the unique way by which you're called to share God's love with the world. It's simply the vehicle.

The incremental change? Ask God to meet you where you are and root you deep in your faith calling, one day at a time. Ask him to lead you through the fear one step at a time as you push into your own vocational calling. Ask him to protect you from finding so much of your identity in vocational success, and instead to use it only as far as it allows you to share his love with the world.

You don't have to change everything overnight. You can begin to correct your course today by making a simple paradigm shift and seeking incremental change.

As you change your paradigm and seek incremental change, trust that God will work in your life one day at a time, and that he'll use your life to establish a legacy of love—a legacy you can pass down to your own children. But as you root into your faith calling, as you teach your children to do the same, understand this, though: It won't be easy. There will be days when you'll feel societal pressure to find your identity in what you do instead of who you are. (I still catch myself doing it.) Your kids will experience it too, especially as they approach adulthood. The cultural currents of vocation and career are strong, especially in developed countries. And the embarrassing truth is, those currents still push and pull John and me, and many of my co-workers. But with intentional effort, through incremental change, I believe we can all live deeper into our faith callings. We can use our particular skills, gifts, and talents to carry the love of God into the world around us.

Because at the end of your life, God won't ask whether you were successful, whether you made a lot of money, or whether you made it to the top. Instead, he'll ask a simple question: Did you know you were loved, and did you use your gifts to spread my love to the world around you? And if you answer, "I did my best, Lord," it's my guess you'll hear the best words.

Well done, good and faithful one.

Afterword

You exited the womb uniquely equipped.

The Master Weaver selected your temperament threads, your character texture, the yarn of your personality, all before you were born. God did not drop you into the world, utterly defenseless and empty-handed. You arrived fully equipped. What motivates you, what exhausts you . . . God authored—and authors—it all.

How would you answer this multiple-choice question?

I am:

_____ a coincidental collision of particles.

_____ an accidental evolution of molecules.

_____ soulless flotsam in the universe.

_____ "fearfully and wonderfully made" (Psalm 139:14 NKJV), "skillfully wrought" (Psalm 139:15 NKJV).

Don't dull your life by missing this point. You are more than statistical chance, more than a marriage of heredity and society; more than a confluence of inherited chromosomes and childhood trauma. More than a walking weathervane, whipped about by the cold winds of fate.

Thanks to God you have been "sculpted from nothing into something" (Psalm 139:15 MESSAGE).

This is the message of the Bible.

And this is the welcome message from Paula Faris in *Called Out*. Each of us is uniquely gifted with what she calls our "faith calling." She urges us to wrestle with important questions like:

Do I understand my faith calling—who I am and my underlying purpose?

Could I write out my faith calling with any sort of clarity?

Do my vocation, my acts of service, my parenting, my side hustle, or my next big idea flow from my faith calling, or is something else steering the ship?

Few questions would be more important than these. And few people would be more qualified to help us find the answers. Paula is incurably curious. She asks astounding questions (I know this firsthand), and she is a wellspring of good advice. (Again, I speak from personal experience.) Most of all, she is in dogged pursuit of a life that lives out faith and values. If you desire to do the same, then you are holding the right book. It is well-written and inviting. The ideas are timely and timeless. Thank you, Paula, for sharing them with us.

—Max Lucado, pastor and bestselling author
of *How Happiness Happens*

Acknowledgments

This could go off the rails in a hurry, because I'm so grateful to so many.

To my husband, John. Thanks for loving me through thick and thin. For loving me when I didn't deserve it. We're together today because you refused to give up on us.

My babies, Caroline, JJ, and Landon—I love you forever.

Mom, you're the best thing that ever happened to Dad and us kids. I love how your little nose goes up, then down, then sideways. Xo.

Dad, losing you felt like my tectonic plates shifting. I miss you every single day. But I know you're still here. Thank you for giving me the gift of perspective, of realizing what's consequential and what's not. Also, Go Blue! (*Please* tell me God is a Michigan Wolverines fan.)

My siblings, Dianne, Mary, and Dan. You've tolerated my incessant questioning since the '70s, and for that you deserve some sort of award. Thank you for nurturing this youngest child, even if it was accompanied by mild torture. Love youuuuuuu.

From the little sister he never had nor wanted, thank you to my dear friend and colleague Dan Harris. My Agnostic-Buddhist friend, you're the one who encouraged me to write this thing. You're also the one who nudged me to launch a faith podcast. Dan, I love you. Now, please eat some bacon.

To the weekend *Good Morning America* team who taught me that highly egotistical news anchors *can* have each other's backs, that we can root for one another. Sara Haines, Ron Claiborne, Rob Marciano, Dan Harris—you have a large piece of my heart and forever will remain the best team I've ever worked with.

Mr. Barsuhn, Mr. Kragel, and Mr. Leightenheimer, thank you for speaking into my vocational calling, and for helping me push past my many fears.

Barbara Fedida for being persistent. Ben Sherwood for believing in me. James Goldston for supporting me.

The amazing team at United Talent Agency—Brandi Bowles and Byrd Leavell, and my agent, Jay Sures—you saw this book for me before I saw it for myself.

My dearest friends on the planet—Krissy, Krysty, and Meredith. Cedarville University brought us together back in the dark ages (1993); the laughter and really bad jokes have kept our friendship going . . . and going. Can't imagine life without you girls!

My colleagues at ABC, *Good Morning America*, and *The View*—thank you for supporting me and this project.

The glam squad who worked legit miracles to capture my personality for this book cover—you're proof that Jesus is still on the throne. Heidi Gutman, Camille Zola, Merylin Mitchell, Jamie Salazar—thanks for making me smile. And keeping me well fed. Xo.

I leaned on so many in the faith community to bring this book to life—Pastors Kent and Alli Munsey (City Church Chicago), Pastors Blaze and Desiree Robertson (Hillsong Connecticut), Max Lucado . . . God gifted you all so uniquely. Thanks for sharing those gifts with me.

Our small group—Whit and Andrea Johnson, Blaze and Desiree. What chapter are we on, again? Ha. I can't believe we get to do life together.

Francesco Bilotto—you've been urging me to write a book for so long. Well, here goes. This one's for you, friend.

Seth Haines—you brought this book to *life*. You provided the words when I had none. You made sense of the nonsensical. You are a literary wonder.

The team at Bethany House Publishers—you took a risk on this first-time author. Andy McGuire, Sharon Hodge, Paul Higdon, Deirdre Thompson, and the entire crew—let's celebrate!

I've always been an open book—just never thought I'd write one! It's been a terrifying yet cathartic experience—putting your heart on paper. So to all who took the time to read this, a massive thank you. I'm beyond grateful.

And finally, Jesus—thank you for your endless grace. For teaching me my value isn't in my vocation. My worth isn't my work. It's about *who I am* not what I do. Everything is for you.

Notes

Chapter 3: Interview with an International Spy: Clarifying Calling

1. "David Shedd," Wikipedia.com, https://en.wikipedia.org/wiki/David_Shedd.
2. Richard Gray, "The Seven Ways You Are Totally Unique," *BBC.com*, January 10, 2017, http://www.bbc.com/future/story/20170109-the-seven-ways-you-are-totally-unique.

Chapter 7: An Impostor in New York

1. Ellen Hendriksen, "What Is Impostor Syndrome?" *Scientific American*, May 27, 2015, https://www.scientificamerican.com/article/what-is-impostor-syndrome/.

Chapter 8: Trading One Identity for Another

1. Carlos Greer, "Paula Faris Is Getting Axed from 'The View,'" *Page Six*, July 20, 2016, https://pagesix.com/2016/07/20/paula-faris-is-getting-axed-from-the-view/.
2. Greer, "Getting Axed."
3. Kelly McLaughlin, "EXCLUSIVE: 'This is a bunch of bull—it's Whoopi's doing.' The View host Paula Faris is cut to one day a week and blames nemesis Goldberg in dressing room meltdown," *DailyMail.com*, August 2, 2016, https://www.dailymail.co.uk/news/article-3718914/.html.

Chapter 9: How Martha Becomes Mary

1. Rebecca Riffkin, "In U.S., 55% of Workers Get Sense of Identity From Their Job," *Gallup*, August 22, 2014, https://news.gallup.com/poll/175400/workers-sense-identity-job.aspx.

About the Author

Paula Faris is a senior national correspondent at ABC News and host of the popular podcast *Journeys of Faith with Paula Faris*, which gives an intimate look at how some of the world's most influential people lean on faith and spirituality in the best and worst of times. An Emmy Award–winning journalist, Paula previously was co-anchor of the *Good Morning America Weekend Edition*, as well as a co-host of *The View*.

Paula began her career behind the scenes: shooting, editing, and producing, spending more than ten years at stations in Chicago, Cincinnati, and Dayton before joining ABC. She's reported on everything from the Inauguration of President Donald Trump to the World Cup in Brazil and the Academy Awards. Her interviews include Hillary Clinton, Joe Biden, Reese Witherspoon, Steph Curry, and the cast of *Avengers*, as well as exclusives with former White House Press Secretary Sean Spicer and Kentucky clerk Kim Davis, who made headlines for refusing to issue marriage licenses to same-sex couples.

A native of Jackson, Michigan, Faris graduated cum laude from Cedarville University in Ohio. She lives in New York with her husband and their three young children, fully aware her value is not in her vocation, reminding herself it's about who we are, not what we do.